HISTORY REPEATED

Block Exchange Quilts by the 19th-Century Patchwork Divas

By Betsy Chutchian and Carol Staehle

"Forever Friendships", a signature quilt made by Charlene Seifert and quilted by Jana Menning, showcases blocks made by the 19th-Century Patchwork Divas in 2000 to commemorate the turn of the 21st century.

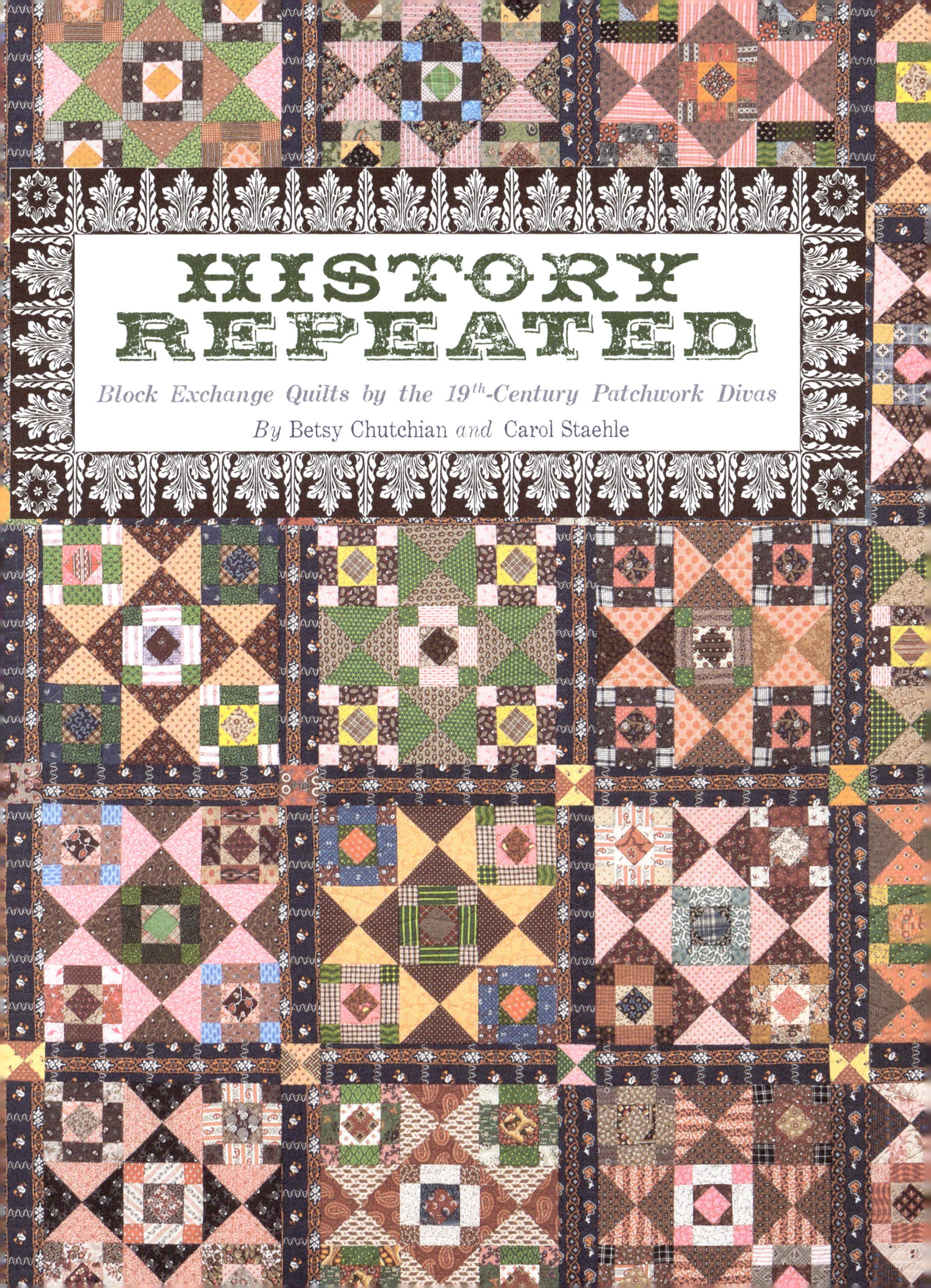

HISTORY REPEATED

Block Exchange Quilts by the 19th-Century Patchwork Divas

By Betsy Chutchian *and* Carol Staehle

HISTORY REPEATED
Block Exchange Quilts by the 19th-Century Patchwork Divas
By Betsy Chutchian and Carol Staehle

EDITOR: Kimber Mitchell
DESIGNER: Bob Deck
PHOTOGRAPHY: Aaron T. Leimkuehler
ILLUSTRATION: Eric Sears
TECHNICAL EDITOR: Christina DeArmond
PRODUCTION ASSISTANCE: Jo Ann Groves

PUBLISHED BY:
Kansas City Star Books
1729 Grand Blvd.
Kansas City, Missouri, USA 64108

All rights reserved
Copyright © 2011 C&T Publishing, Inc.

Kansas City Star Quilts is an imprint of C&T Publishing, Inc., P.O. Box 1456, Lafayette, CA 94549. ctpub.com

No part of this book may be reproduced, stored in a retrieval system, or transmitted in any form or by any means, electronic, mechanical, photocopying, recording or otherwise, without prior consent of the publisher.

First edition, first printing
ISBN: 978-1-935362-91-3

Library of Congress Control Number: 2011929477

POD Edition

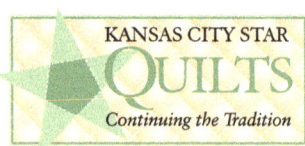 

ACKNOWLEDGMENTS

We have many people to thank for helping to make this book a reality. Our thanks go to:

Rhonda Weddle for her computer skills and tremendous help in typing our text.

Annette Plog, a sister Patchwork Diva, for her assistance at the photo shoot, computer skills, and willingness to step in and help at a moment's notice.

The Westport Historical Society and **Alana Smith** for allowing us to use the Society's headquarters—the beautiful 1855 Harris-Kearney House—for our location photography.

Bettina Havig for the use of her Pyramids quilt photo.

Bobbie Aug for permission to use her quilt as our inspiration for the Wheel of Fortune block exchange.

Steve Chutchian for his patience in driving us to Kansas City for the photo shoot, hauling the quilts in and out of the vehicle, and hanging the quilts in the photo studio. Thank you for being tall!

To our Kansas City Star team, who made our book wonderful:

Kimber Mitchell, our editor, for her attention to detail and for keeping us on task.

Bob Deck, our designer, for putting the pieces of this book together so beautifully.

Eric Sears, our illustrator, for the helpful diagrams.

Christina DeArmond, our technical editor, for checking our measurements.

Jo Ann Groves, our production assistant, for making sure the photos were picture-perfect.

And most especially to our photographer **Aaron Leimkuehler** for his skillful eye and his patience with us while we were getting all the quilts ready for photography.

DEDICATION

This book is lovingly dedicated to our sister **19th-Century Patchwork Divas**. The common thread of quilting has held our group together for more than 13 years as we've watched our children grow, leave home, marry, and have children of their own. We have been there for each other during life's crises, and our friendship and love have been the glue that has held us together.

TABLE OF CONTENTS

About the Authors	Page 6
The 19th-Century Patchwork Divas	Page 7
Introduction	Page 8
How to Run a Successful Block Exchange	Page 9
Fabric Swatchbook	Page 10
Antique Flying Geese	Page 11
Double Nine-Patch	Page 19
Pyramids	Page 30
Nine-Patch Pinwheels	Page 39
Hourglass	Page 51
Carolina Lily	Page 63
Blindman's Fancy	Page 75
Wheel of Fortune	Page 85
Cheddar Triangles	Page 97
Ohio Stars	Page 105

ABOUT THE AUTHORS

Betsy Chutchian (above right) and Carol Staehle (above left) met through the Quilter's Guild of Arlington, Texas, more than 20 years ago. They quickly formed a friendship through their common interests in quilting, love of traditional quilts, and appreciation of antique quilts.

Carol began her sewing journey making clothes at age 12. Both of her grandmothers quilted but the quilting gene skipped a generation. Although she was a lifelong sewer, Carol's mother never made a quilt but she nurtured her daughter's love of sewing. She gave Carol her first sewing machine, a Singer featherweight, which she still has today. After graduating from Purdue University with a teaching degree, Carol taught Language Arts and English for junior and senior high school students in Michigan, Iowa, and Ohio.

She took a quilting class in the mid-1980s and hasn't looked back since. In the mid-1990s, Carol began teaching quiltmaking classes at her local quilt shop in Arlington, Texas. An award-winning quilter, she currently leads a monthly quilt club at Cabbage Rose Quilting and Fabrics in Fort Worth, Texas. Carol and her husband John live in Arlington, Texas, and have a son, Jim, daughter-in-law, Pon, granddaughter, Clarrisa, and two cats.

As a child learning to sew on her two grandmothers' treadle sewing machines, Betsy fell in love with fabric and quilts. In 1980, she received a B.A. in History from the University of Texas in Arlington and taught herself to quilt after receiving a quilt top made by a great aunt and great grandmother. This began a passionate journey combining her love of fabric, quiltmaking, and history.

A former quilt shop owner, Betsy has taught quiltmaking at a number of quilt shops since 1990 and she has traveled across Texas, sharing her love of 19th-century quilts through lectures, trunk shows, and workshops since 2004. She leads a monthly club at Lone Star House of Quilts in Arlington, Texas. In 2010, Betsy's first reproduction fabric line was printed with Blue Hill Fabrics and a second in 2011.

In addition to quilting, Betsy enjoys cooking, antiquing, and collecting antique quilts. She and her husband Steve live in Grand Prairie, Texas. They have a daughter, Rachel, son, Matt, son-in-law, Craig, and three cats.

THE 19TH-CENTURY PATCHWORK DIVAS

The 19th-Century Patchwork Divas are a block exchange group that recreates antique quilts by trading traditional blocks made with 1800s reproduction fabrics. For several years, we were simply known as a block exchange group. Then in 2003, one member wrote an article about our group for *Quilters Newsletter* magazine and in anticipation of its publication, we selected the appropriate name: 19th-Century Patchwork Divas.

Our quilts were first displayed in 2003 for a special exhibit at the Quilter's Guild of Arlington show. In 2004 and 2008, they were displayed in Houston at the International Quilt Festival. The quilts from that 2008 display then traveled to exhibits in Chicago, Pittsburgh, and Long Beach, California. The Patchwork Divas' quilts have also been exhibited at the Trinity Valley Quilt Guild's quilt show in 2008 and 2010 and the Rocky Mountain Quilt Museum in Golden, Colorado, in 2009. Several Patchwork Divas' quilts have also been published in national quilt magazines.

Originally, all our group members lived in the Dallas/Fort Worth area, but through the years, some moved out of the area and new members have joined our quilting circle. We currently have 22 members and hold a yearly retreat.

Back row, left to right: Sonja Kraus, Arlington, TX; Linda Wilkey, Mathis, TX; Diana Petterson, Washington, D.C.; Marilyn Mowry, Irving, TX; Arlene Heintz, Waxahachie, TX; Ann Jernigan, Arlington, TX; Deb Otto, Hurst, TX; Annette Plog, Arlington, TX; Mary Freeman, Schertz, TX. *Front row, left to right:* Alice Harvey, Arlington, TX; Carol Staehle, Arlington, TX; Betsy Chutchian, Grand Prairie, TX; Karen Hodges, Midlothian, TX. Current members not pictured: Betty Edgell, Colleyville, TX; Charlene Seifert, Arlington, TX; Janet Henderson, Fort Worth, TX; Jean Johnson, Murphy, TX; Karen Roxburgh, Arvada, CO; Peggy Morton, Boerne, TX; Ramona Williams, Missouri City, TX; Sue Troyan, Virginia Beach, VA; and Wanda Hetrick, Arlington, TX

CHARTER MEMBERS: Betsy Chutchian; Carol Staehle; Alice Harvey; Annette Plog; Arlene Heintz; Betty Edgell; Deb Otto; Diana Petterson; Paula Barnes, Katy, TX; Sue Troyan; and Wanda Hetrick

INACTIVE MEMBERS: Paula Barnes; Sharon Cheng, Fort Worth, TX; and Fawn Crossland, Chesapeake, VA

Introduction

The 19th-Century Patchwork Divas began in 1997 as a conversation between us—two friends who shared a fondness for old quilts. For several years prior to the group's start, we had talked about forming a circle of quilters who enjoyed making traditional quilts with the newly available reproduction fabrics at that time. What began as a small gathering of friends has grown into a 22-member group connected by our mutual passion for antique quilts of the 19th century.

We are inspired by the designs, blocks, and fabrics in the quilts that 19th-century women used to comfort their families and beautify their homes. From the simplicity of the utilitarian quilt made for everyday use to the more elaborate one reserved for special occasions, the 19th-Century Patchwork Divas find a wealth of block ideas for our exchanges.

For this book, we've selected some of our favorite block exchanges from past years. They represent a variety of styles and degrees of difficulty. The chapters are arranged chronologically, reflecting our group's growth from simpler blocks in the early years to more complex ones in our more recent past. Over time, we became more particular about fabric selections, eventually adhering to specific historical time periods for our exchanges.

This book features quilts by each of our members. Our exchanges begin with their suggestions based on inspiration gleaned from a variety of sources such as antique quilts and quilt tops they own, state documentation records, and museum books. Each Patchwork Diva may choose how to set her blocks. Some prefer to reproduce the antique inspiration quilt, following the colors and fabric patterns as closely as possible. Others simply want to capture the feel and era of the quilt in a different setting. And yet others create entirely unique quilts that may even be contemporary in appearance.

No matter what approach you prefer, you'll find lots of inspiration in this book's 10 different block designs. Each chapter also features 1–3 setting options to complete your quilts. To give you even more setting and color palette ideas, most of the chapters also include a gallery of additional quilts that showcase that same block design. We hope you enjoy these selections from our past block exchanges!

Betsy   *Carol*

HOW TO RUN A SUCCESSFUL BLOCK EXCHANGE

The first and most important rule when organizing a block exchange is to gather a group of friends with common interests, sewing skills, and work ethics. As co-founders of the 19th-Century Patchwork Divas, we invited friends who also admired antique quilts and 1800s reproduction fabrics. Of this group, most were quilting teachers and all had similar sewing skills.

As a starting point for our exchanges, our group uses an antique quilt for inspiration. Often it is the block itself that sparks inspiration as in the Antique Flying Geese and Double Nine Patch quilts. The simplicity of these blocks offered quick piecing methods as well as several fabric choices and setting variations.

Establishing fabric guidelines for each exchange is an important ingredient for success. If you want to focus on a particular era, choose reproduction fabrics that reflect that time period. Making blocks to suit a certain era is challenging and fun. Because fabric choices will vary by participant, quilts will naturally have that scrappy look of so many 19th-century quilts. For our early exchanges, the Patchwork Divas did not require members to use 1800s reproduction fabrics from a specific period within that century. Instead, we could use any 1800s reproduction print. Because an increasing number of reproduction fabric collections now specify their particular eras, our group has become more selective about requiring a certain time period for the exchanges.

Once your group decides which fabrics to use and the number of blocks to make, divide the number of blocks by the number of participants to determine how many different blocks each member will need to make. Part of the beauty of the exchange format is that making the blocks in sets goes faster than if you were to make them individually.

Then set a due date for completing the blocks. Be sure to set a reasonable timeframe and stick with the deadlines. It is also important to set a date for members to drop out or join the exchange so that all participants can purchase adequate yardage in a timely fashion and avoid getting duplicate blocks when a member drops out unexpectedly.

Every group needs an enforcer, and for the Patchwork Divas, it is Carol. While we set the rules for each exchange together, Carol is the one who keeps everyone on track, and the members appreciate that. Without a strong structure of rules and limitations, the resulting exchange of blocks can be disappointing.

PROLIFIC PATCHWORK

Since the start of the 19th-Century Patchwork Divas, our members have participated in 45 block exchanges. Multiply that number by the number of participating members in each exchange and the result is a potential 530 exchange quilts, which all begin with a bag of blocks for each participant. From those 530 bags, we have completed 275 quilts and pieced 87 quilt tops. And for future years, we have 158 bags of blocks just waiting to be made into quilts. Given our 45 exchanges, 275 finished quilts is quite an accomplishment!

FABRIC
SWATCHBOOK

More than 10 years ago, one of our members came up with a great way of documenting the fabrics she used for our exchanges. She cut out a small sample from each piece of reproduction fabric she purchased for her quilt, then glued them into a small notebook organized by color. When other Patchwork Divas saw her swatchbook, they started creating their own!

To start your own swatchbook, cut a 2" square of fabric and glue it to acid-free paper. For ease, we like to use the kind with pre-punched holes (available at office supply stores). We prefer to organize our swatches by fabric collection, noting the collection's name, the fabric designer and/or the manufacturer, and most importantly for an historical group like ours, the collection's time period. For easy reference, use a different notebook for each time period. Possible period groupings might be 1775-1825, 1826-1865, and 1866-1900.

These swatchbooks have been an invaluable tool in our exchanges. At a glance, we can see which fabrics would be suitable for a particular project, and our newer members love to use them for identifying fabrics.

CHAPTER 1
ANTIQUE FLYING GEESE

Inspiration for this December 2000 exchange was the many antique strippy quilts with Flying Geese units in their strips and the simplicity of the block itself. Seventeen participants exchanged eight Flying Geese blocks each for a total of 136 blocks. Fabric selection was early to mid-1800s reproduction fabrics. For the "geese" fabrics, we chose interesting medium- to large-scale prints and avoided tone-on-tone and miniature prints. For the "sky" (background) fabrics, we selected shades of beige and tan.

FLYING GEESE BLOCK

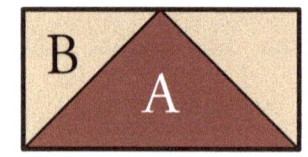

Finished block size: 4" x 8"

CUTTING INSTRUCTIONS

For four blocks, cut:
- 1—9¼" square (A) from medium to dark prints for "goose" fabric. Then cut the square in half twice diagonally from corner to corner
- 4—4⅞" squares (B) from beige to tan prints for "sky" fabric. Then cut squares in half once diagonally from corner to corner

BLOCK ASSEMBLY

Sew two B triangles to a larger A triangle. Press to sky. Repeat for the other three Flying Geese blocks.

ANTIQUE FLYING GEESE: SPIRAL SET

FABRIC REQUIREMENTS

Blocks:
- 2 yards total of assorted light prints in beige and tan
- 2 yards total of assorted medium- to large-scale dark prints

Sashing:
- 2¼ yards brown floral

Backing:
- 5 yards fabric of your choice

Binding:
- ⅔ yard brown print

CUTTING INSTRUCTIONS

From assorted light prints in beige and tan, cut:
- 90—4⅞" squares. Then cut the squares in half once diagonally from corner to corner

From assorted medium- to large-scale dark prints, cut:
- 23—9¼" squares. Then cut the squares in half twice diagonally from corner to corner

From brown floral, cut:
- 8—4½" x 78" strips lengthwise for sashing and borders. From these strips, cut the dimensions listed in the assembly diagram on page 17, starting with the longest lengths. Label each strip

From brown print, cut:
- 8—2½" strips the width of fabric for double-fold binding (To give our quilts an antique look, we prefer a 1⅛"-wide single-fold binding. Nineteenth-century quilts often had narrow binding)

SEWING INSTRUCTIONS

1. Referring to the block assembly instructions on page 12, make 90 Flying Geese units.

2. Referring to the first diagram on page 16, sew a strip of six Flying Geese. Then sew a 4½" x 24½" brown floral sashing strip (A) to the right of it.

3. Referring to the second diagram on page 16, sew a 4½" x 12½" brown floral sashing strip (B) to the top of the unit from Step 2. Then sew a strip of three Flying Geese to the bottom.

4. Referring to the third diagram on page 16, sew a 4½" x 36½" brown floral sashing strip (C) to the left of the unit from Step 3. Then sew a strip of nine Flying Geese to the right of it.

5. Referring to the fourth diagram on page 16, sew a 4½" x 24½" brown floral sashing strip (D) to the bottom of the unit from Step 4. Then sew a strip of six Flying Geese to the top of it.

6. Referring to the fifth diagram on page 16, sew a 4½" x 48½" brown floral sashing strip (E) to the right of the unit from Step 5. Then sew a strip of 12 Flying Geese to the left of it.

7. Referring to the sixth diagram on page 16, sew a 4½" x 36½" brown floral sashing strip (F) to the top of the unit from Step 6. Then sew a strip of nine Flying Geese to the bottom of it.

8. Referring to the seventh diagram on page 16, sew a 4½" x 60½" brown floral sashing strip (G) to the left of the unit from Step 7. Then sew a strip of 15 Flying Geese to the right of it.

9. Referring to the eighth diagram on page 16, sew a 4½" x 48½" brown floral sashing strip (H) to the bottom of the unit from Step 8. Then sew a strip of 12 Flying Geese to the top of it.

10. Referring to the ninth diagram on page 16, sew a 4½" x 72½" brown floral sashing strip (I) to the right of the unit from Step 9. Then sew a strip of 18 Flying Geese to the left of it.

11. Referring to the assembly diagram on page 17, sew a 4½" x 60½" brown floral sashing strip (J) to the top of the unit from Step 10.

12. Referring to the assembly diagram on page 17, sew a 4½" x 76½" brown floral sashing strip (K) to the left of the unit from Step 11.

13. Quilt, bind, and enjoy. Arlene's quilt is machine-quilted with diagonal lines in the "sky", curves in the "geese", and an outline that follows the design of the sashing fabric.

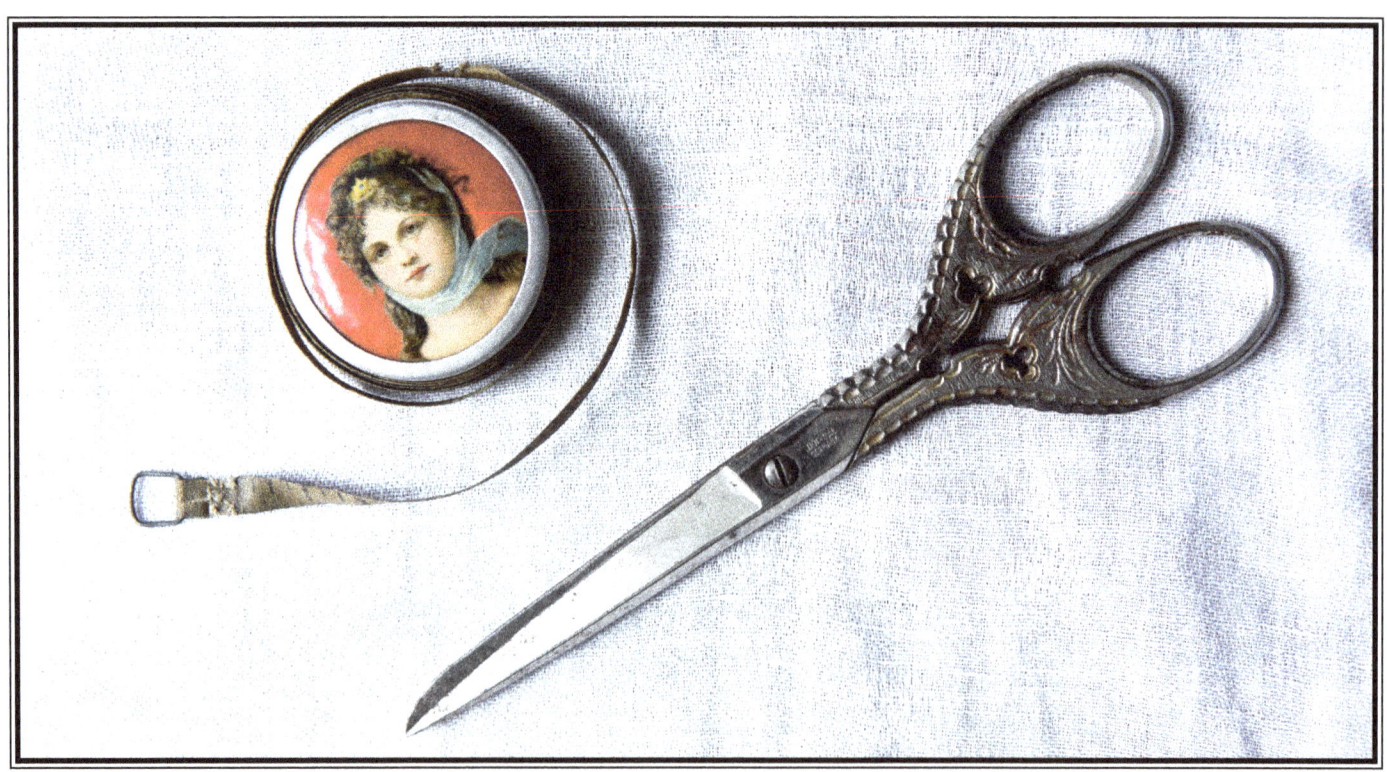

Spiraling Flying Geese

Made by Arlene Heintz of Waxahachie, Texas
Quilted by Dana Goyer of Euless, Texas
Finished size: 64" x 76"
Finished block size: 4" x 8"
Number of blocks needed: 90

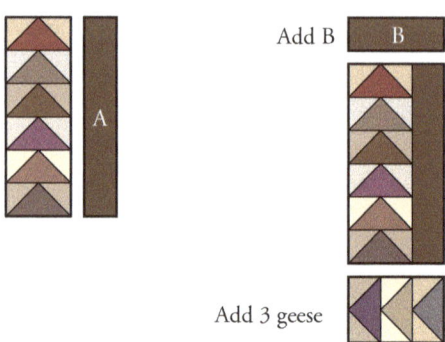

Add B

Add 3 geese

Add C   Add 9 geese

Add 6 geese

Add D

Add 12 geese   Add E

Add F

Add 9 geese

Add G   Add 15 geese

Add 12 geese

Add H

Add 18 geese   Add I

16 HISTORY REPEATED

Assembly Diagram

HISTORY REPEATED

GALLERY

Antique Flying Geese

Made by Deb Otto of Euless, Texas
Quilted by Dawn Smith of Grapevine, Texas
Finished size: 76" x 95"
20 blocks in a Flying Dutchman set
Each block is made of eight Flying Geese units. 1½"-wide sashing strips are then added on all four sides of the block, making it 19" square finished.
Quilting: Baptist Fan design

Flying North

Made and hand-quilted by Jean Johnson of Murphy, Texas
Finished size: 87½" x 82½"
126 blocks in a strippy set
Outer border and interior strips were cut according to the width of the stripe fabric and a secondary fabric was added for visual interest
Quilting: All-over chevron design with perle cotton

Texas Bound

Made by Sue Fowler Troyan of Virginia Beach, Virginia
Quilted by Rosemary Skinner of Virginia Beach, Virginia
Finished size: 96½" x 106½"
138 blocks in a sashed diagonal set
Quilting: Feathers and a compass design in one corner

CHAPTER 2
DOUBLE NINE-PATCH

Inspiration for this April 2002 block exchange was the block itself. Its simplicity presents many different setting options. Nineteen participants exchanged fourteen 3" finished nine-patch blocks each for a total of 266 blocks. Fabric selection was limited to brown prints for the corners and centers of the nine-patch blocks. For lights, we used only creams, tans, and shirtings with either brown or black motifs. Duplicate blocks were acceptable for this exchange.

DOUBLE NINE-PATCH BLOCK

Finished block size: 9" x 9"

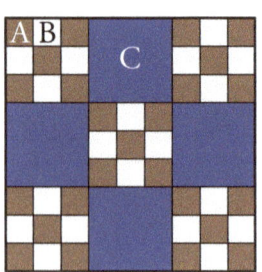

CUTTING INSTRUCTIONS

For each Double Nine-Patch block, cut:
- 25—1½" squares (A) from dark prints for nine-patch units
- 20—1½" squares (B) from light prints for nine-patch units
- 4—3½" squares (C) from medium prints for unpieced squares

BLOCK ASSEMBLY

1. Sew 5—1½" dark print squares (A) and 4—1½" light print squares (B) together to create a nine-patch block.

2. Sew five nine-patch blocks to four medium print squares. Press to the unpieced squares.

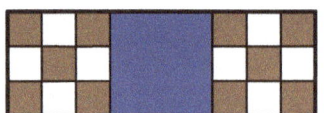

DOUBLE NINE-PATCH: ON-POINT SET

FABRIC REQUIREMENTS

Blocks:
- 1⅛ yard total of assorted light prints for nine-patch units
- 1½ yards total of assorted brown prints for nine-patch units
- 1⅜ yards total of indigo prints for unpieced squares

Setting squares, setting triangles, corner triangles, and borders:
- 4¼ yards indigo print (this should be a different print than the one listed in the block yardage above)

Backing:
- 5½ yards fabric of your choice

Binding:
- ⅔ yard indigo print

CUTTING INSTRUCTIONS

From assorted brown prints, cut:
- 750—1½" squares (A) for nine-patch units

From assorted light prints, cut:
- 600—1½" squares (B) for nine-patch units

From indigo prints, cut:
- 120—3½" squares (C) for unpieced squares

From indigo print 2, cut:
- 5—9½" strips the width of fabric for setting squares. Then sub-cut these strips into 20—9½" squares
- 2—14" strips the width of fabric for setting triangles. Then sub-cut these strips into 5—14" squares and cut twice diagonally from corner to corner
- 2—7¼" squares for corner triangles. Then cut these squares once diagonally from corner to corner
- 8—8½" strips the width of fabric for border
- 9—2½" strips the width of fabric for double-fold binding (To give our quilts an antique look, we prefer a 1⅛"-wide single-fold binding. Nineteenth-century quilts often had narrow binding)

SEWING INSTRUCTIONS

1. Referring to the block assembly instructions on page 20, make 30 Double Nine-Patch blocks.

2. Referring to the assembly diagram on page 24, arrange the Double Nine-Patch blocks, setting squares, setting triangles, and corner triangles in diagonal rows. Then sew the rows together. Press to the setting squares.

3. Measure your quilt top through the center from top to bottom. Then join the lengths of the 8½"-wide indigo print border strips to match that measurement. Sew these strips to the sides of the quilt top. Press to the border.

4. Measure your quilt top from side to side. Join the lengths of the 8½"-wide indigo print border strips to match that measurement. Sew these strips to the top and bottom of the quilt top. Press to the border.

5. Quilt, bind, and enjoy. Using a stencil with a design from the 1840s, Betsy hand-quilted her quilt with perle cotton and a utility stitch.

Indigo Double Nine-Patch

Made and hand-quilted by Betsy Chutchian of Grand Prairie, Texas
Finished size: 79½" x 92⅛"
Finished block size: 9" x 9"
Number of blocks needed: 30

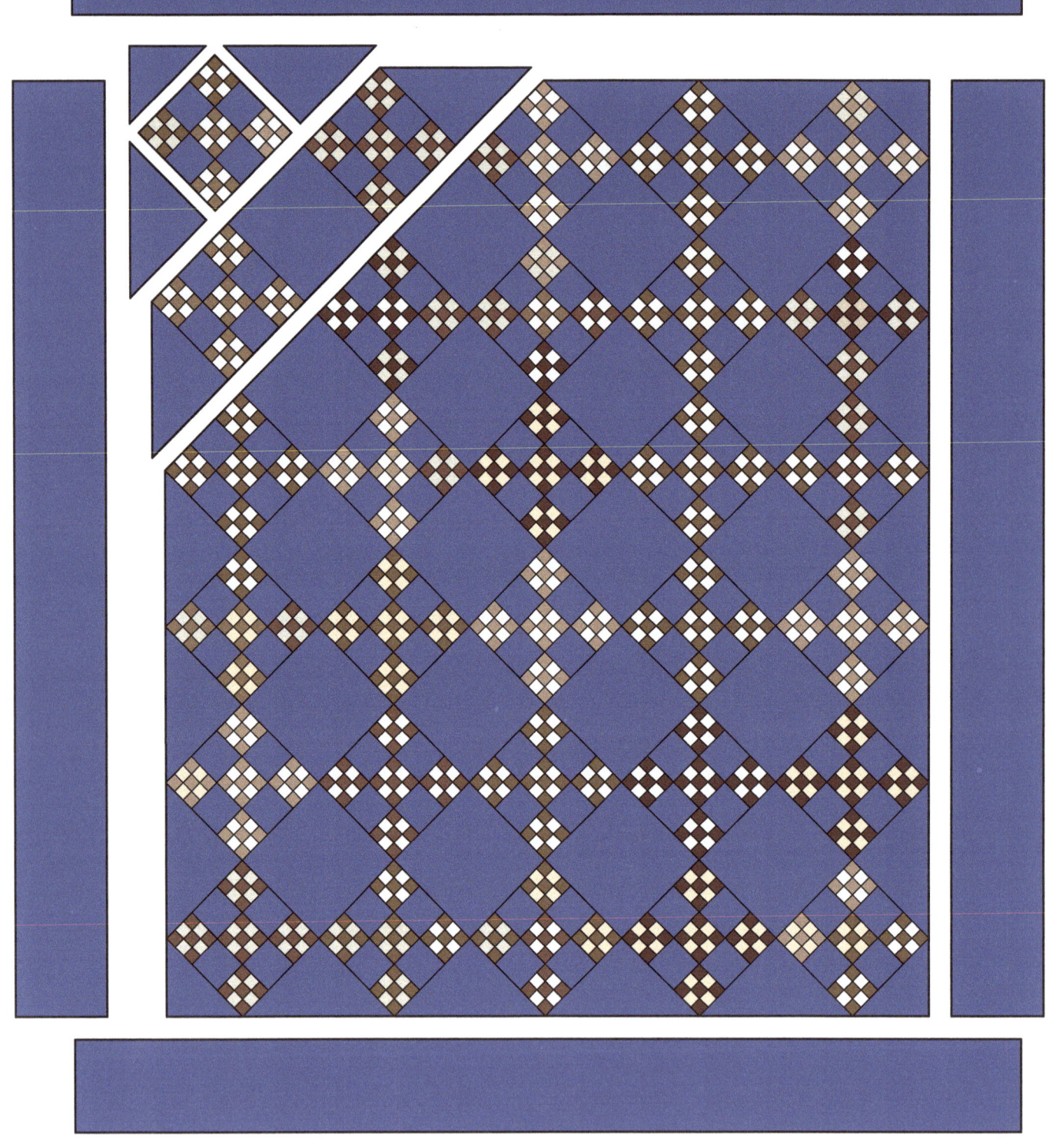

Assembly Diagram

DOUBLE NINE-PATCH: SASHED SET

FABRIC REQUIREMENTS

Blocks:
- 2 yards total of assorted light and cream prints for nine-patch units
- 2¼ yards total of assorted brown prints for nine-patch units
- 1¾ yards total of brown or madder prints for unpieced squares

Sashing:
- 2½ yards brown or madder stripe

Backing:
- 5½ yards fabric of your choice

Binding:
- ⅔ yard brown or brown stripe

CUTTING INSTRUCTIONS

From brown prints, cut:
- 1330—1½" squares (A) for 3" nine-patch blocks and pieced cornerstones

From light or cream prints, cut:
- 1064—1½" squares (B) for 3" nine-patch blocks and pieced cornerstones

From brown or madder stripes, cut:
- 168—3½" squares (C) for unpieced squares
- 9—9½" strips the width of fabric for sashing. Then sub-cut these strips into 97—3½" x 9½" strips
- 9—2½" strips the width of fabric for double-fold binding (To give our quilts an antique look, we prefer a 1⅛"-wide single-fold binding. Nineteenth-century quilts often had narrow binding)

SEWING INSTRUCTIONS

1. Referring to the block assembly instructions on page 20, make 42 Double Nine-Patch blocks.

2. Referring to the block assembly instructions for the nine-patch units on page 20, make 56—3" finished nine-patch blocks for the cornerstones.

3. Referring to the assembly diagram on page 28, arrange the Double Nine-Patch blocks, sashing strips, and cornerstones.

4. Sew the block rows together with six blocks and seven sashing strips. Repeat to create a total of seven rows.

5. Sew the sashing rows together with seven nine-patch blocks and six sashing strips. Repeat to create a total of eight rows.

6. Referring to the assembly diagram on page 28, sew the rows from Steps 4 and 5 together. Press to the sashing.

7. Quilt, bind, and enjoy. Karen machine-quilted a grid in the pieced blocks and straight lines in the sashing.

Baum Chocolate Box

Made and machine-quilted by Karen Roxburgh of Arvada, Colorado
Finished size: 72" x 88"
Finished block size: 9" x 9"
Number of blocks needed: 42

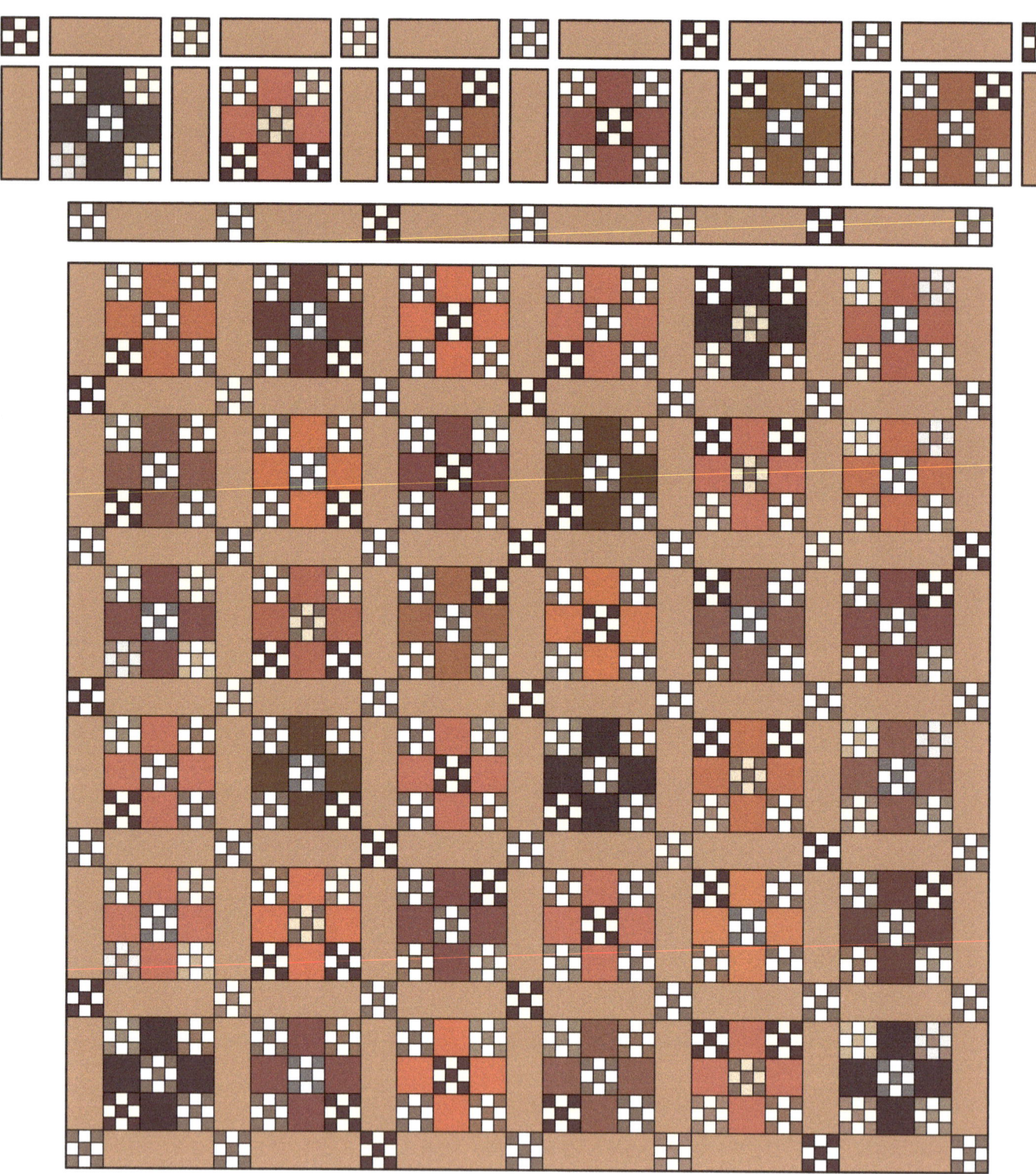

Assembly Diagram

28 HISTORY REPEATED

GALLERY

Chrome and Brown Double Nine-Patch 👉

Made and hand-quilted by Annette Plog of Arlington, Texas
Finished size: 66" x 84"
32 blocks in a straight set
Borders are 3"-wide finished
Quilting: Baptist Fan with perle cotton and a utility stitch

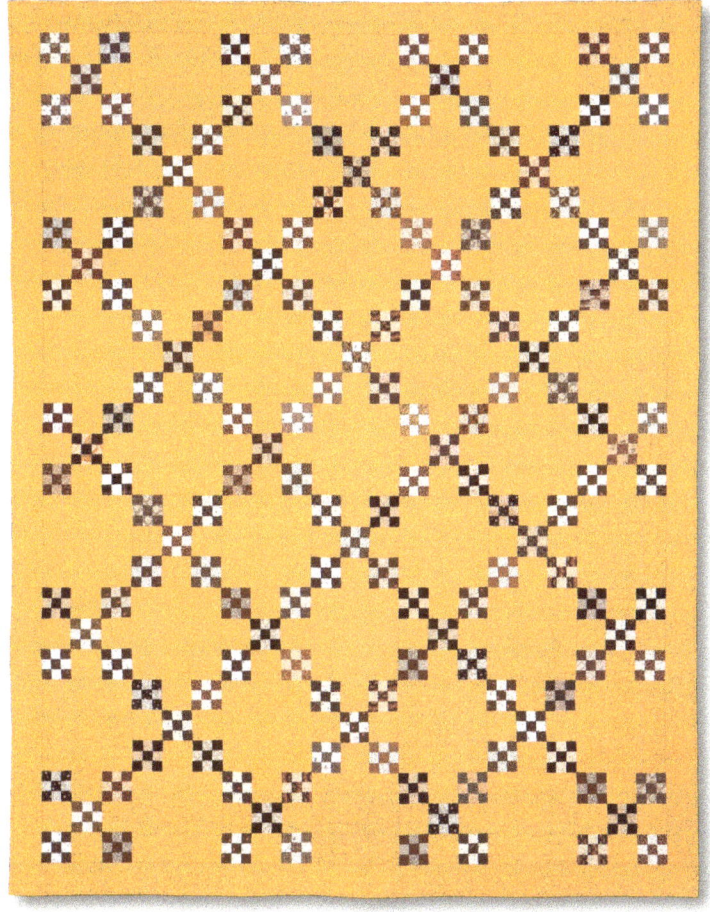

👈 Chocolate Covered Cherries and Berries

Made by Janet Henderson of Fort Worth, Texas
Quilted by Sheri Mecom of Bedford, Texas
Finished size: 71" x 81"
56 blocks in a sashed set
Green sashing strips are 1"-wide finished
Quilting: Clamshell design in blocks and straight lines in the sashing

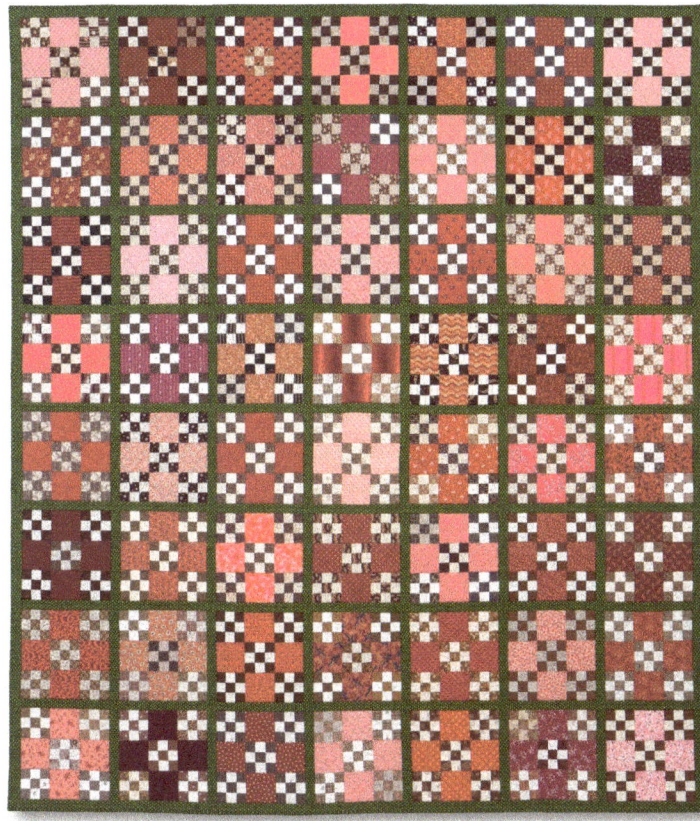

CHAPTER 3
PYRAMIDS

Inspiration for this September 2003 block exchange was a quilt made by Bettina Havig that was exhibited at the Trinity Valley Quilters' Guild Show in Fort Worth, Texas. Fifteen participants exchanged eight blocks each for a total of 120 blocks. Fabric selection was 1800s reproduction fabrics in medium to dark values. Each triangle in the pyramid had to be a different fabric.

PYRAMIDS BLOCK

Finished block size: 5¼" x 6⅛" (at base)

CUTTING INSTRUCTIONS

For each block, cut:

- 9 – 2½" equilateral triangles from dark and medium prints. These can be cut using the 60-degree angle on your ruler or one of several 60-degree ruler tools available. If you prefer to use a template, use template A on page 32.

BLOCK ASSEMBLY

1. To make row 2, sew three triangles together. Press.

2. Sew one triangle to the top of row 2. Press.

3. To make row 3, sew five triangles together. Press.

4. Sew the unit from Step 2 to the top of the unit from Step 3, matching the point in the middle of the rows. Press.

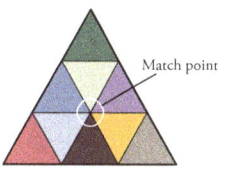

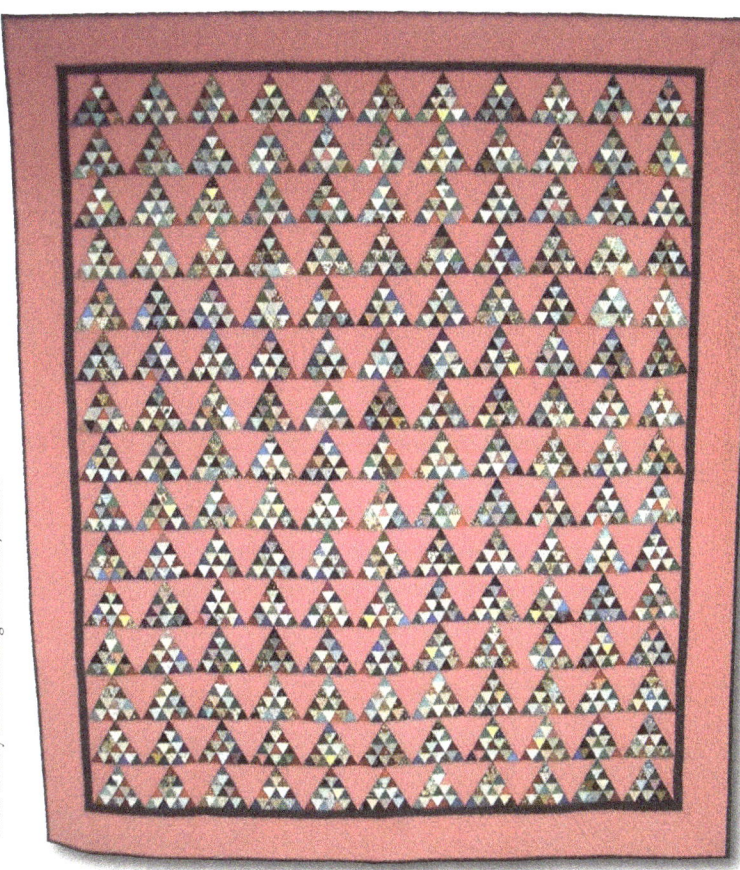

This quilt made by Betting Havig inspired the Pyramids quilt block exchange.

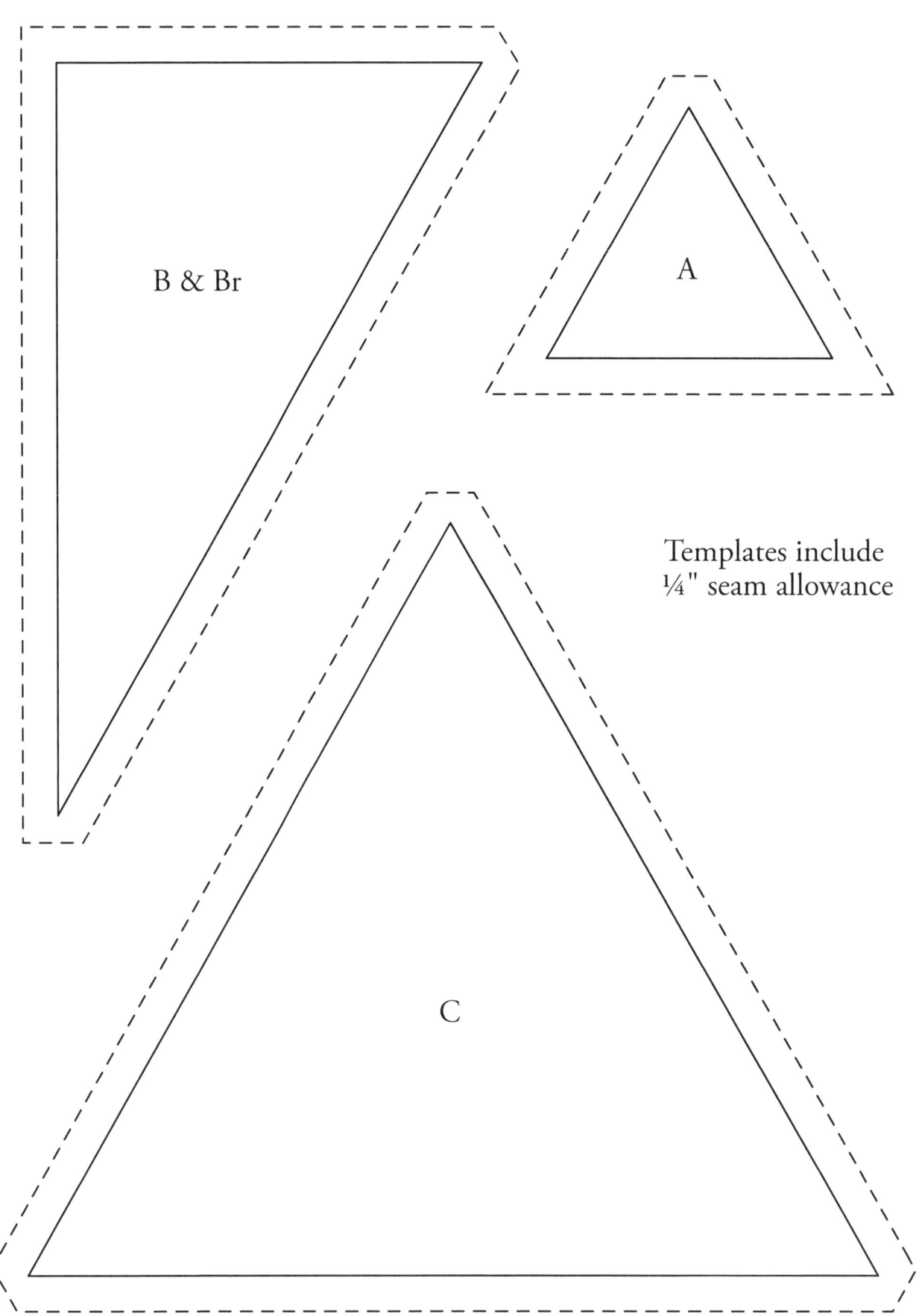

PYRAMIDS: STRAIGHT SET

FABRIC REQUIREMENTS

Blocks:
- 3 yards total of assorted medium and dark prints

Setting triangles and outer border:
- 5 yards of gold print

Inner border:
- ⅔ yard green print

Backing:
- 8¼ yards fabric of your choice

Binding:
- ⅔ yard gold print

CUTTING INSTRUCTIONS

From assorted medium and dark prints, cut:
- 1260 – 2½" equilateral triangles. These can be cut using the 60-degree angle on your ruler or one of several 60-degree ruler tools available. If you prefer to use a template, use template A on page 32

From gold print, cut:
- 12—5¾" strips the width of fabric for nonpieced pyramids. Then cut 126 from template C
- 14 half pyramids from template B
- 14 half pyramids from template BR (the reverse of template B)
- 8—6½" strips the width of fabric for outer border
- 9—2½" strips the width of fabric for double-fold binding (To give our quilts an antique look, we prefer a 1⅛"-wide single-fold binding. Nineteenth-century quilts often had narrow binding)

From green print, cut:
- 8—2½" strips the width of fabric for inner border

SEWING INSTRUCTIONS

1. Referring to the block assembly instructions on page 31, make 140 pyramid blocks.

2. Sew 14 rows of 10 pieced pyramid blocks and 9 unpieced alternating pyramids, starting and ending with a pieced pyramid. Press to the unpieced pyramids.

3. Referring to the previous diagram, sew a half pyramid block B at the beginning of each of the 14 rows and a half pyramid block BR at the end of each of the 14 rows. Press.

4. Referring to the assembly diagram on page 36, arrange the 14 rows completed in Step 3. Then sew the rows together.

5. Measure your quilt top through the center from top to the bottom. Join the lengths of 2½"-wide green print inner border strips to match your measurement. Sew the strips to the sides of the quilt top. Press to the border.

6. Measure your quilt top through the center from side to side. Join the lengths of 2½"-wide green border strips to match your measurement. Sew the strips to the top and bottom of your quilt top. Press to the border.

7. Repeat Steps 5 and 6 for the gold print outer border strips.

8. Quilt, bind, and enjoy. Diana hand-quilted a Baptist fan design over the quilt's surface with perle cotton and a utility stitch.

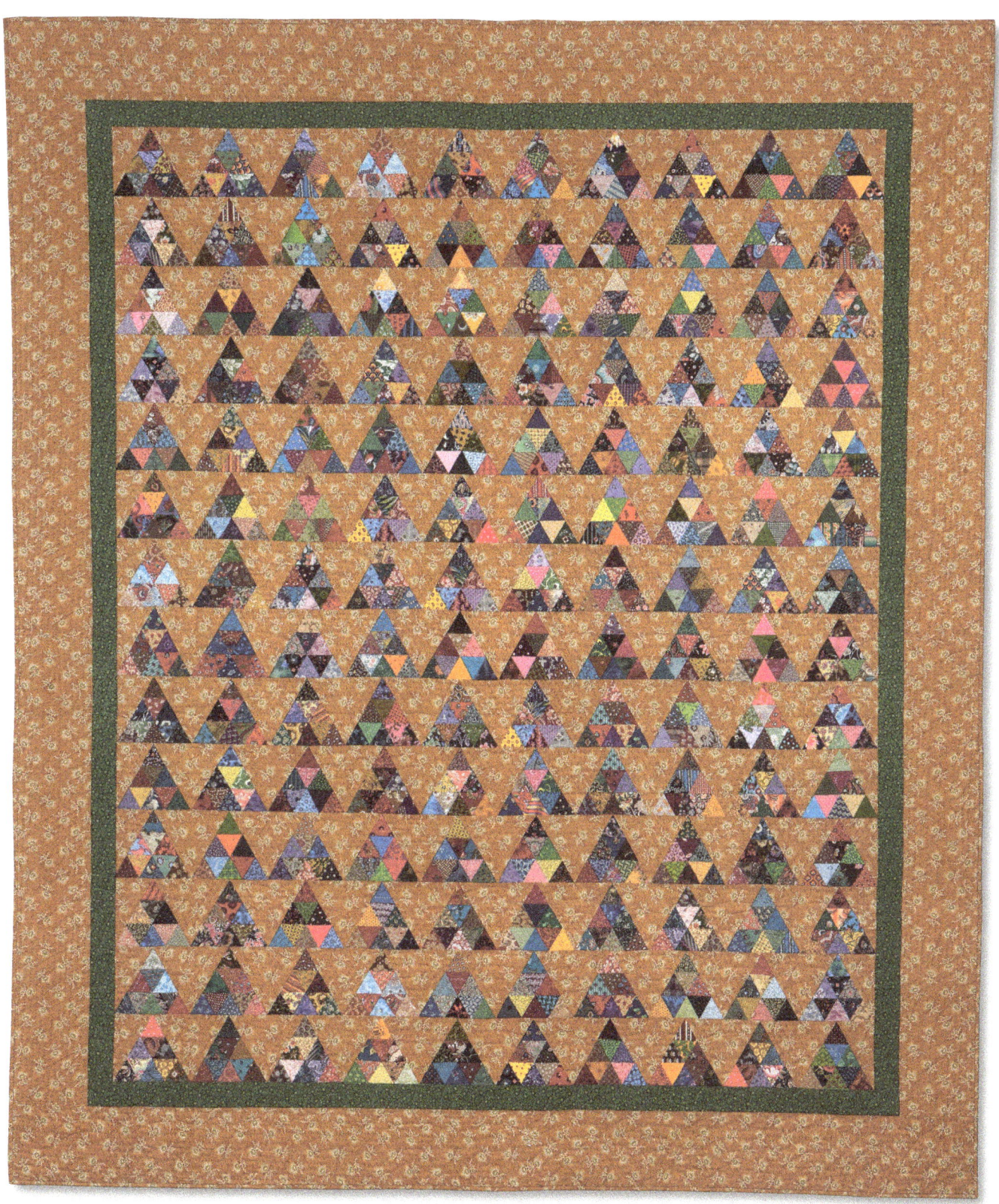

Antique Diva Pyramids

Made and hand-quilted by Diana Petterson of Washington, D.C.
Finished size: 77¼" x 89½"
Finished block size: 5¼" tall x 6⅛" wide (at base)
Number of blocks needed: 140

HISTORY REPEATED

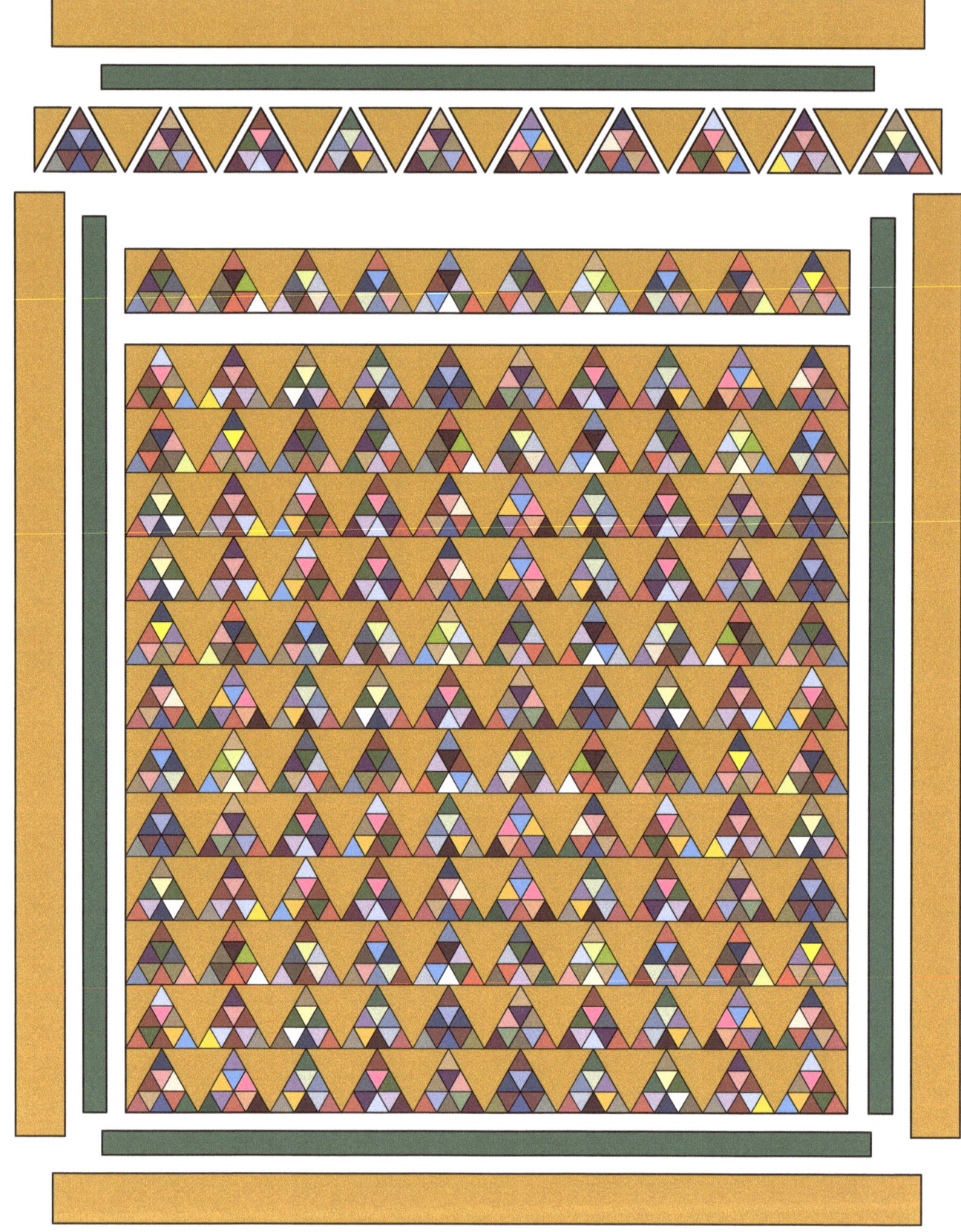

Assembly Diagram

36 HISTORY REPEATED

GALLERY

Pink Pyramids

Made and hand-quilted by Annette Plog of Arlington, Texas
Finished size: 72" x 75"
120 blocks in a straight set
Blocks alternate with nonpieced pyramids
Inner border is 1"-wide finished and the outer border is 6"-wide finished
Quilting: Overall clamshell

Almost 1000 Pyramids

Made by Betsy Chutchian of Grand Prairie, Texas
Quilted by Sheri Mecom of Bedford, Texas
Finished size: 46½" x 58"
945—60-degree triangles and 52—60-degree half triangles in a straight set
Quilting: Diagonal lines through quilt center and feathered pattern in borders

HISTORY REPEATED 37

Pyramids with Attitude

Made by Ramona Bailey Williams of Missouri City, Texas
Quilted by Melba Drennan of Pearland, Texas
Finished size: 61" x 75"
90 blocks
Quilting: Echo of the diamond design

Scrappy Pyramids

Made and hand-quilted by Janet Henderson of Fort Worth, Texas
Finished size: 78¾" x 84"
96 blocks in a strippy set
Setting strips are 6"-wide finished
Quilting: Chevron design with a utility stitch

CHAPTER 4: NINE-PATCH PINWHEELS

Inspiration for this September 2004 block exchange was an antique quilt top owned at the time by Arlene Heintz and currently owned by Jo Morton. Nineteen participants exchanged four blocks each for a total of 76 blocks. Fabric selection was reproduction prints in all colors except purples since the antique inspiration quilt had very few of those shades. We chose small- and medium-scale prints.

NINE-PATCH PINWHEELS BLOCK

Finished block size: 6" x 6"

CUTTING INSTRUCTIONS

For each block, cut:
- 10—1⅞" squares (A) from light print. Then cut squares once diagonally from corner to corner
- 10—1⅞" squares (B) from dark print. Then cut squares once diagonally from corner to corner
- 4—2½" squares (C) from medium print

BLOCK ASSEMBLY

1. Sew a light print triangle to a dark print triangle to create a half-square triangle unit. Repeat to make a total of 20 of these units. To make the construction of the half-square triangles go faster, you can use 1" finished triangle paper instead of sewing triangles together. (If using 1" triangle paper to create your half-square triangle units, you will need 10 paper squares. Right sides together, layer your light and medium fabrics. Then pin the paper in place on top and sew on the dotted lines with a short stitch length. Cut units apart on solid lines and remove paper. Press to the dark print. Then trim dog-ears).

2. Sew four half-square triangle units together to create a pinwheel unit. Repeat to make a total of five of these.

3. Assemble five pinwheel units and four 2½" medium print squares to create a block.

An antique quilt top owned by Jo Morton inspired the Nine-Patch Pinwheels block exchange.

NINE-PATCH PINWHEELS: ON-POINT SET

FABRIC REQUIREMENTS

Blocks:
- 2 yards total of assorted light prints for pinwheel units
- 2 yards total of assorted dark prints for pinwheel units
- 1½ yards total of assorted medium prints for unpieced squares

Setting squares, setting triangles, zigzag border, and outer border:
- 4¾ yards gray print
- 1⅛ yard red print for zigzag border

Backing:
- 7½ yards fabric of your choice

Binding:
- ⅔ yard gray print

CUTTING INSTRUCTIONS

From light print, cut:
- 640—1⅞" squares (A). Then cut squares once diagonally from corner to corner

From dark print, cut:
- 640—1⅞" squares (B). Then cut squares once diagonally from corner to corner

From medium print, cut:
- 256—2½" squares (C)

From gray print, cut:
- 9 —6½" strips the width of fabric for setting squares. Then sub-cut into 49—6½" squares
- 2 —9¾" strips the width of fabric for side setting triangles. Then sub-cut into 7—9¾" squares. Then cut each square twice diagonally from corner to corner
- 2—5⅛" squares for corner triangles. Then cut squares once diagonally
- 19—2" strips the width of fabric for the inner zigzag border. Then sub-cut into 372—2" squares (these include the 4—2" squares needed for the corners of the zigzag border)
- 2 —3⅞" squares for zigzag border corner triangles. Then cut squares once diagonally from corner to corner
- 8—4½" strips the width of fabric for the outer border
- 9— 2½" strips the width of fabric for double-fold binding (To give our quilts an antique look, we prefer 1⅛"-wide single-fold binding. Nineteenth-century quilts often had narrow bindings)

From red print, cut:
- 10—3½" strips the width of fabric for zigzag border. Then sub-cut strips into 184—2" x 3½" rectangles
- 2—3⅞" squares for zigzag border corners. Then cut squares once again diagonally from corner to corner

Nine-Patch Pinwheels

Made and hand-quilted by Carol Staehle of Arlington, Texas
Finished size: 82" x 82"
Finished block size: 6" x 6"
Number of blocks needed: 64

SEWING INSTRUCTIONS

Quilt center:

1. Referring to the block assembly instructions on page 40, make 64 Nine-Patch Pinwheel blocks (To make the pinwheel units, we recommend using 1" finished triangle paper).

2. Referring to the assembly diagram on page 45 arrange the Nine-Patch Pinwheel blocks, setting squares, setting triangles, and corner triangles in diagonal rows. Sew the units within the rows together. Then sew the rows together. Press to the setting squares.

Inner border:

1. Draw a diagonal line from corner to corner on the wrong side of a 2" gray print square. With right sides together, layer the marked 2" gray print square on top of a 2" x 3½" red print rectangle. Then sew on the drawn line. Press the triangle back and trim away excess fabric below, leaving a ¼" seam allowance.

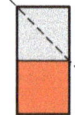 

2. Repeat Step 1 for the opposite end of the 2" x 3½" red print rectangle.

3. Make 92 units as created in Step 2 and 92 mirror image units of them.

4. Using a full ¼" seam allowance, sew the units from Steps 2 and 3 into 23 pairs and press the seams open to create one inner zigzag side border strip. Measure your quilt top through the center from top to bottom. The zigzag border will probably be slightly larger, in which case you will need to take an additional ¹⁄₁₆" seam allowance in 4-6 seams for the border to fit properly. It is best to spread out these adjustments throughout the length of the strip rather than in consecutive seams. Repeat for the remaining three inner border strips, but for the top and bottom strips, measure your quilt top through the center from side to side.

5. Draw a diagonal line once from corner to corner on the wrong side of a 3⅞" gray print square. With right sides together, layer the marked gray square on top of the 3⅞" red print square to create a half-square triangle unit. Sew a ¼" seam on both sides of the drawn line. Cut the square apart on the drawn line. Press to the dark print. Repeat this entire step to make a total of 4 half-square triangle units.

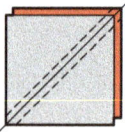 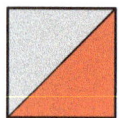 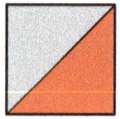

6. Draw a diagonal line on the wrong side of the four 2" gray print squares. Then layer one of these 2" gray print squares in the lower right corner of each half-square triangle unit from Step 5. Sew on the drawn line. Press to the corner, then trim excess fabric below.

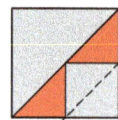 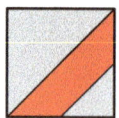

7. Referring to the assembly diagram on page 45, sew two finished units from Step 6 to opposite ends of the top and bottom inner zigzag border strips.

8. Referring to the assembly diagram, sew the zigzag side border strips to the sides of the quilt top. Press seams to the pieced top.

9. Referring to the assembly diagram, sew the remaining zigzag border strips to the top and bottom of the quilt top. Press seams to the pieced top.

Outer border:

1. Measure your quilt top through the center from top to bottom. Then join the 4½"-wide gray outer border strips to match your measurement. Referring to the assembly diagram on page 45, sew these strips to the sides of the quilt top. Press to the border.

2. Measure your quilt top through the center from side to side. Then join the 4½"-wide gray outer border strips to match your measurement. Referring to the assembly diagram, sew these strips to the top and bottom of the quilt top. Press to the border.

3. Quilt, bind, and enjoy. Carol's quilt was hand-quilted using perle cotton and a utility stitch with a grid in the pieced center and a Baptist Fan design through the red zigzag border and the gray outer border.

Assembly Diagram

HISTORY REPEATED 45

NINE-PATCH PINWHEELS: STRAIGHT SET

FABRIC REQUIREMENTS

Blocks and sashing cornerstones:
- 3 yards total of assorted light prints for pinwheels and sashing cornerstones
- 3 yards total of assorted dark prints for pinwheels and sashing cornerstones
- 2 yards total of assorted medium prints for unpieced squares

Sashing and borders:
- 1 yard light print for block sashing
- 2 yards red print for sashing and inner border
- 1⅝ yards brown print for outer border

Backing:
- 8¼ yards fabric of your choice

Binding:
- ¾ yard brown print

CUTTING INSTRUCTIONS

From light print, cut:
- 1,032—1⅞" squares (A). Then cut squares once diagonally from corner to corner (32 of these squares will be used for pinwheel cornerstones)
- 4—6½" strips the width of fabric. Then sub-cut strips into 100—1½" x 6½" rectangles for block sashing

From assorted medium and dark prints, cut:
- 1,032—1⅞" squares (B) from medium print. Then cut squares once diagonally from corner to corner (32 of these squares will be used for pinwheel cornerstones)
- 400—2½" squares (C) from dark print
- 25—1½" squares for block sashing

From red print, cut:
- 3—13½" strips the width of fabric. Then sub-cut strips into 40—2½" x 13½" rectangles for sashing
- 8—2½" strips the width of fabric for inner border

From brown print, cut:
- 8—6½" strips the width of fabric for outer border
- 10—2½" strips the width of fabric for double-fold binding (To give our quilts an antique look, we prefer a 1⅛"-wide single-fold binding. Nineteenth-century quilts often had narrow binding)

SEWING INSTRUCTIONS

1. Referring to the block assembly instructions on page 40, make 100 Nine-Patch Pinwheel blocks. To speed up the piecing process, we recommend using triangle paper to create the half-square triangle units.

2. Make 16—2" finished pinwheel blocks for the red sashing cornerstones by joining four half-square triangle units as shown.

3. Sew a Nine-Patch Pinwheel block to opposite sides of a 1½" x 6½" block sashing strip. Repeat to create a second row. Then sew a 1½" x 6½" block sashing strip to opposite sides of a 1½" square cornerstone. Then join the three rows. Press to the sashing.

4. Repeat Step 3 to create a total of 25 blocks. Sew five of these blocks and four 2½" x 13½" red print sashing strips to create a row. Repeat to create a total of five rows.

5. Sew four of the 2" finished pinwheel blocks created in Step 2 to five 2½" x 13½" red print sashing strips. Repeat to create a total of four rows.

Nine-Patch Pinwheels

Made by Deb Otto of Euless, Texas
Quilted by Dawn Smith of Grapevine, Texas
Finished size: 89" x 89"
Block size: 6" x 6"
Number of blocks needed: 100

6. Referring to the assembly diagram below, arrange the nine rows assembled in Steps 4 and 5. Then sew the rows together. Press to the sashing.

7. Measure your quilt top through the center from top to bottom. Then join the 2½"-wide red inner border strips to match your measurement. Sew these strips to the sides of the quilt top. Press to the border.

8. Measure your quilt top through the center from side to side. Then join the 2½"-wide red inner border strips to match your measurement. Sew these strips to the top and bottom of the quilt top. Press to the border.

9. Repeat Steps 7 and 8 for the 6½"-wide outer border strips.

10. Quilt, bind, and enjoy. Each Nine-Patch Pinwheel in Deb's quilt is quilted individually and the outer border is quilted in half wreaths.

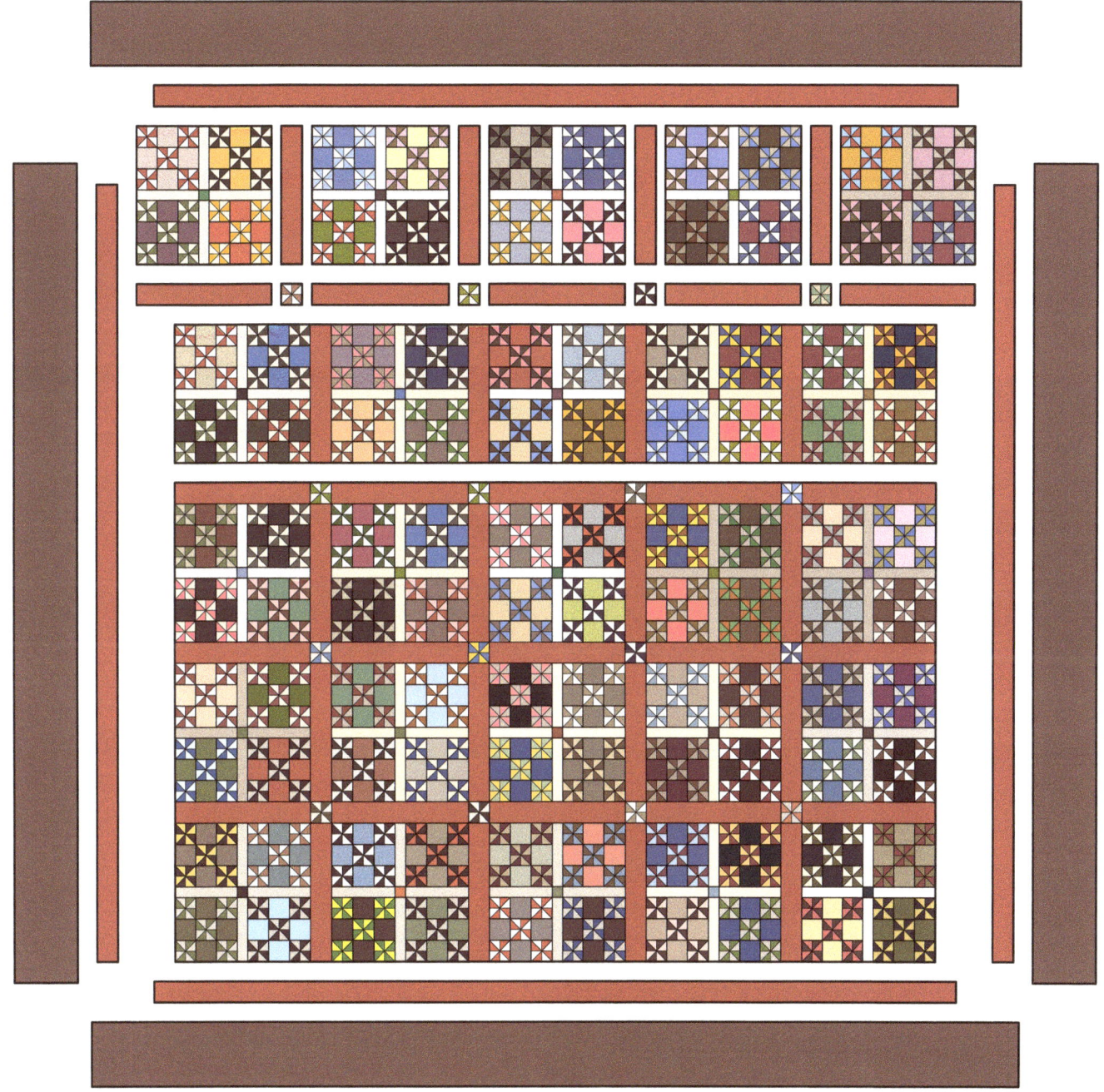

Assembly Diagram

HISTORY REPEATED 49

GALLERY

Wheel of Nines

Made by Jean Johnson of Murphy, Texas
Machine-quilted by John Liddicoat of McKinney, Texas
Finished size: 81" x 90"
72 blocks in a sashed on-point set
Brown sashing is 1"-wide finished and
setting red squares are 6" square finished
Quilting: Feathered wreaths in alternating red squares
and half wreaths in setting triangles

Nine-Patch Pinwheels

Made by Marilyn Mowry of Irving, Texas
Hand-quilted by Irene Sander of Lowden, Iowa
Finished size: 59½" x 76"
63 blocks in an on-point set
Quilting: In-the-ditch and an antique reproduction motif in the alternate squares

CHAPTER 5
HOURGLASS

Inspiration for this 2005 block exchange was an antique quilt top owned by Patchwork Diva Arlene Heintz. Sixteen participants exchanged 42 blocks per person for a total of 672 blocks. Fabric selection was clarets, indigos, shirtings, conversational prints, reds, browns, blacks, and muddy greens.

HOURGLASS BLOCK

Finished block size: 3" x 3"

CUTTING INSTRUCTIONS

For two blocks, cut:
- 1—4½" square from light to medium print. These are oversized for trimming later
- 1—4½" square from medium to dark print. These are oversized for trimming later

BLOCK ASSEMBLY

1. Draw a diagonal line once from corner to corner on the wrong side of the light to medium print square. With right sides together, layer the light to medium print square on top of the medium to dark print square. Sew a ¼" seam on both sides of the drawn line. Cut apart on the drawn line. Press to the dark print.

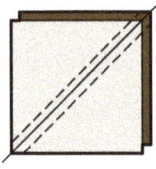 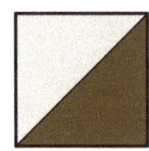 

2. With right sides together, layer two half-square triangle units on top of each other. Draw a line from corner to corner. Then sew a ¼" seam allowance on both sides of the drawn line. Then cut on the drawn line. Press and trim blocks to 3½" square.

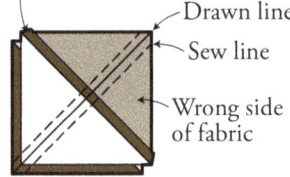  

PATCHWORK DIVA TIP:

To reduce bulk under the block, clip the seam intersection as shown and press to the dark fabrics. This makes the seams nest together smoothly.

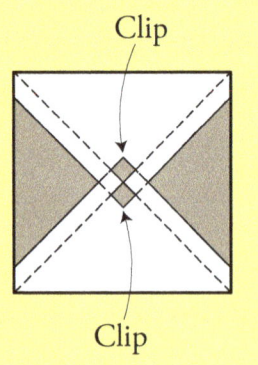

This 1890s antique quilt top owned by Arlene Heintz sparked inspiration for the Hourglass block exchange.

HOURGLASS: STRAIGHT SET

FABRIC REQUIREMENTS

Blocks:
- 4½ yards total of assorted light to medium prints
- 4½ yards total of assorted dark prints

Backing:
- 4½ yards fabric of your choice

Binding:
- ⅔ yards blue print

CUTTING INSTRUCTIONS

From assorted light to medium prints, cut:
- 280—4½" squares. These are oversized for trimming later

From medium to dark prints, cut:
- 280—4½" squares. These are oversized for trimming later

From blue print, cut:
- 8—2½" strips the width of fabric for double-fold binding (To give our quilts an antique look, we prefer a 1⅛"-wide single-fold binding. Nineteenth-century quilts often had narrow binding)

SEWING INSTRUCTIONS

1. Referring to the block assembly instructions on page 52, make 560 Hourglass blocks.

2. Sew two Hourglass blocks together, alternating the position of the blocks so that light triangles are next to dark triangles as shown below. Repeat to create a second unit.

3. Sew the two units from Step 2 together.

4. Repeat Steps 2 and 3 to make a total of 140 units shown in Step 3.

5. Sew the units from Step 4 into larger blocks of 16 hourglass units each. Repeat to create a total of 35 blocks.

6. Referring to the assembly diagram on page 56 sew the units from Step 5 into seven rows of five blocks each.

7. Quilt, bind, and enjoy. Marilyn's quilt is machine-quilted in a Texas Fan design.

Hourglass

Made by Marilyn Mowry of Irving, Texas
Quilted by Sheri Mecom of Bedford, Texas
Finished size: 60" x 84"
Finished block size: 3" x 3"
Number of blocks needed: 560 Hourglass blocks

Assembly Diagram

HOURGLASS: MEDALLION SET

FABRIC REQUIREMENTS

Broken Dishes and Hourglass blocks:
- 3 yards total of assorted light prints
- 3 yards total of assorted dark prints

Central medallion block:
- You will need a large block or a framed smaller block of your choice that measures 18" square finished

Border:
- 2 yards brown print

Backing:
- 5½ yards fabric of your choice

Binding:
- ⅝ yard brown print

CUTTING INSTRUCTIONS

From assorted light prints, cut:
- 80—4½" squares for 3" finished Hourglass blocks. These are oversized for trimming
- 64—4" squares for 6" Broken Dishes blocks. Then cut once diagonally from corner to corner. These are oversized for trimming

From assorted dark prints, cut:
- 80—4½" squares for 3" finished Hourglass blocks. These are oversized for trimming
- 64—4" squares for 6" finished Broken Dishes blocks. Then cut once diagonally from corner to corner. These are oversized for trimming

From brown print, cut:
- 4—6½" strips lengthwise for border
- 8—2½" strips the width of fabric for double-fold binding (To give our quilts an antique look, we prefer a 1⅛"-wide single-fold binding. Nineteenth-century quilts often had narrow binding)

SEWING INSTRUCTIONS

1. Referring to the block assembly instructions on page 52, make 160—3" square finished Hourglass blocks. Trim blocks to measure 3½" unfinished.

2. Sew 16 Hourglass blocks into a larger block. Repeat to make a total of four of these blocks.

3. Referring to the two units to the left and right of the central block of your choice in the assembly diagram on page 59, sew 24 Hourglass blocks into a larger block. Repeat to make a total of four of these blocks.

4. Referring to the assembly diagram on page 59 sew together the eight units from Steps 2 and 3 and a central medallion block of your choice.

5. Sew a light print triangle cut from the 4" squares and a dark print triangle cut from the 4" squares to create a half-square triangle unit. Press to the dark triangle. Then trim to measure 3½". Repeat this to make a total of four half-square triangle blocks. Sew the blocks together to complete a 6" square finished Broken Dishes block.

 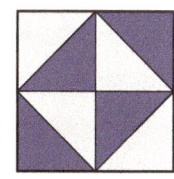

6. Repeat Step 5 to create a total of 32—6" square finished Broken Dishes blocks.

7. Sew seven 6" square finished Broken Dishes blocks together to create a row for the side border. Repeat to create a second row for the other side border.

 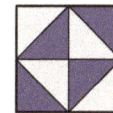 

HISTORY REPEATED 57

8. Sew nine 6" square finished Broken Dishes blocks together to create a row for the top border. Repeat to create a second row for the bottom border.

9. Referring to the assembly diagram on page 59, sew the four rows from Steps 7 and 8 to the quilt center.

Hourglass

Made and quilted by Carol Staehle of Arlington, Texas
Finished size: 66" x 66"
Finished block size: 3" x 3" and 6" x 6"
Number of blocks needed: 160–3" Hourglass blocks and 32–6" Broken Dishes blocks

10. Measure through the center of your quilt top from top to bottom. Then cut two lengths of 6½"-wide brown print strips to match your measurement. Sew these two strips to the sides of your quilt top.

11. Measure through the center of your quilt top from side to side. Then cut two lengths of 6½"-wide brown print strips to match your measurement. Sew these two strips to the top and bottom of your quilt top.

12. Quilt, bind, and enjoy. Carol quilted a grid through the quilt center and a cable design in the border.

Assembly Diagram

HISTORY REPEATED 59

HOURGLASS: ON-POINT SET

FABRIC REQUIREMENTS

Blocks:
- 5 yards total of assorted light prints
- 5 yards total of assorted dark prints

Backing:
- 4½ yards fabric of your choice

Binding:
- ⅔ yards brown print

CUTTING INSTRUCTIONS

From assorted light prints, cut:
- 240—4½" squares for 3" finished Hourglass blocks
- 72—3½" squares for 2" finished Hourglass blocks
- 34—3" squares for Half Hourglass blocks. Then cut squares once diagonally from corner to corner

From assorted dark prints, cut:
- 240—4½" squares for 3" finished Hourglass blocks
- 72—3½" squares for 2" finished Hourglass blocks
- 34—3" squares for Half Hourglass blocks. Then cut squares once diagonally from corner to corner

From brown print, cut:
- 10—2½" strips the width of fabric for double-fold binding (To give our quilts an antique look, we prefer a 1⅛"-wide single-fold binding. Nineteenth-century quilts often had narrow binding)

SEWING INSTRUCTIONS

1. Referring to the block assembly instructions on page 52, make 480 Hourglass blocks. Trim to 3½" square.

2. Referring to the block assembly instructions on page 52, make 144 Hourglass blocks. Trim to 2½" square.

3. Sew together a light print Half Hourglass triangle and a dark print Half Hourglass triangle to make a Half Hourglass triangle unit. Repeat to make a total of 68 of these.

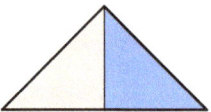

4. Referring to the assembly diagram on page 62, sew together 8 rows of 9—3" finished Hourglass blocks each to create unit A. Repeat to make a total of four of these.

5. Referring to the assembly diagram on page 62, sew together 6 rows of 6—2" finished Hourglass blocks each to create unit B. Repeat to make a total of four of these.

6. Referring to the assembly diagram on page 62, sew together 36—3" finished Hourglass blocks and 9 Half Hourglass blocks to create a setting triangle (unit C). Repeat to make a total of four of these.

7. Referring to the assembly diagram on page 62, sew together 12—3" finished Hourglass blocks and 8 Half Hourglass blocks to create a corner triangle (unit D). Repeat to make a total of four of these.

8. Referring to the assembly diagram, sew together the units from Steps 4-7 in rows to create the quilt top.

9. Quilt, bind, and enjoy. Betsy's quilt is quilted in an all-over paisley design.

Hourglass

Made by Betsy Chutchian of Grand Prairie, Texas
Quilted by Sheri Mecom of Bedford, Texas
Finished size: 72¼" x 72¼"
Number of blocks needed: 480–3" finished Hourglass blocks,
144–2" finished Hourglass blocks, and 68 Half Hourglass blocks

Assembly Diagram

62 HISTORY REPEATED

CHAPTER 6
CAROLINA LILY

Inspiration for this April 2006 block exchange was a circa-1880 North Carolina Lily quilt in the International Quilt Study Center in Lincoln, Nebraska. Twenty participants exchanged two blocks each for a total of 40 blocks. Fabric selection included browns, madder reds, and indigos as well as background prints in cream to tan.

CAROLINA LILY BLOCK

Finished block size: 9" x 9"

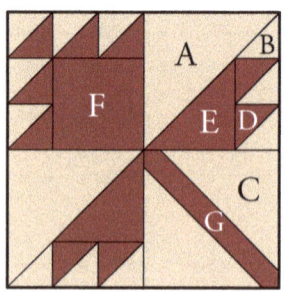

CUTTING INSTRUCTIONS

For one block, cut:
- 1—5⅜" square (A) from light background print. Then cut once diagonally from corner to corner
- 1—2⅜" square (B) from light background print. Then cut once diagonally from corner to corner
- 1—5" square (C) from light background print. Then cut once diagonally from corner to corner
- 5—2½" squares (D) from light background print
- 5—2½" squares (D) from dark print
- 1—3⅞" square (E) from dark print. Then cut once diagonally from corner to corner
- 1—3½" square (F) from dark print
- 1—1⅛" x 7" rectangle (G) from dark print for stem

BLOCK ASSEMBLY

1. Draw a diagonal line once from corner to corner on the wrong side of the 2½" light background print square. With right sides together, layer the light background print square on top of a 2½" dark print square. Sew a ¼" seam on both sides of the drawn line. Cut on the drawn line. Press to the dark print. Then trim the half-square triangle units to measure 2". For multiple blocks, we recommend using a 1½" finished triangle paper product to create your half-square triangle units.

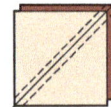  

2. Sew a row of three half-square triangle units and a row of two half-square triangle units. Then sew the row of two half-square triangle units to the left of a 3½" dark print square. Then sew the row of three half-square triangle units to the top of the previously pieced unit.

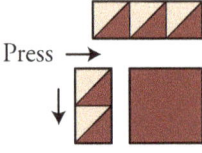 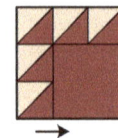

3. Sew an A triangle to the right of the finished unit in Step 2 and another A triangle to the base of it.

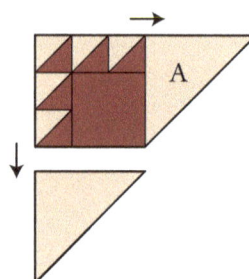

4. Sew two half-square triangle units together then sew a B triangle to the left of that row. Then sew an E triangle to the top of that unit.

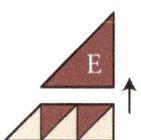

5. Sew two half-square triangle units together, then sew a B triangle to the top of that row. Then sew an E triangle to the left of that row.

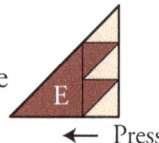

6. Sew a C triangle to both sides of a G strip. Note that the stem is oversized. Press to stem. Trim the unit to 5" square.

7. Sew the unit from Step 6 to the bottom of the unit from Step 5 and the right of the unit from Step 4.

8. Referring to the previous diagram, sew the finished unit from Step 3 to the unit from Step 7.

Inspiration Quilt

The Carolina Lily block exchange was inspired by this circa-1880 North Carolina Lily quilt. It was probably made in Indiana County, Pennsylvania, and features primarily hand piecing.

CAROLINA LILY: SASHED DIAGONAL SET

FABRIC REQUIREMENTS

Blocks:
- 3 yards total of assorted light prints
- 2½ yards total of assorted dark prints

Sashing:
- 3¼ yards green print
- 3¼ yards pink print (There will be twice as much pink left over as the green. We suggest using the remainder for a pieced backing)

Backing:
- 8 yards fabric of your choice

Binding:
- ¾ yard green print

CUTTING INSTRUCTIONS

From assorted light prints, cut:
- 42—5⅜" squares (A). Then cut once diagonally from corner to corner
- 40—2⅜" squares (B). Then cut once diagonally from corner to corner
- 40—5" squares (C). Then cut once diagonally from corner to corner
- 210—2½" squares (D)

From assorted dark prints, cut:
- 210—2½" squares (D)
- 40—3⅞" squares (E). Then cut once diagonally from corner to corner
- 42—3½" squares (F)
- 40—1⅛" x 7" rectangles (G)

From green print, cut:
- 18—2" x 115" strips lengthwise for sashing
- 10—2½" strips the width of fabric for double-fold binding (To give our quilts an antique look, we prefer a 1⅛"-wide single-fold binding. Nineteenth-century quilts often had narrow binding)

From pink print, cut:
- 9—2" x 115" strips lengthwise for sashing

SEWING INSTRUCTIONS

1. Referring to the block assembly instructions on page 64, make 32 Carolina Lily blocks.

2. Referring to Steps 2 and 3 of the block assembly instructions on page 64, create a flower-top half block. Repeat to create a total of 8 of these.

3. Referring to Steps 4-7 of the block assembly instructions on page 64, create a flower-bottom half block. Repeat to create a total of 8 of these.

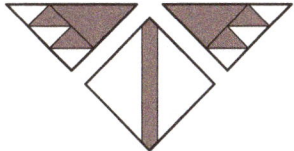 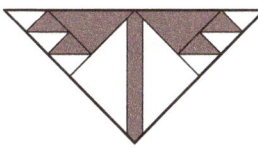

4. Referring to Steps 2 and 3 of the block assembly instructions on page 64, create a flower-top quarter block. Cut the block ¼" to the left of the center. You will only use the section with the ¼" seam allowance.

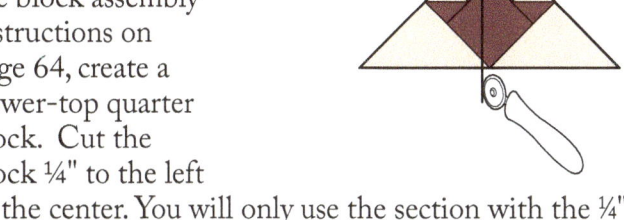

Cut ¼" to the left of center

5. Referring to Steps 2 and 3 of the block assembly instructions on page 64, create a flower-top quarter block. Cut the block ¼" to the right of the center. You will only use the section with the ¼" seam allowance.

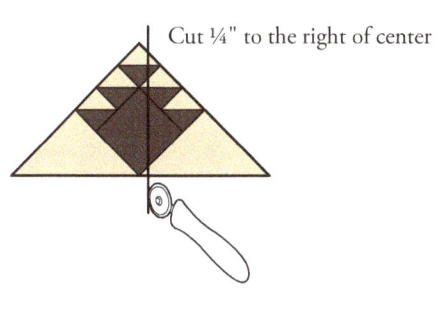

Cut ¼" to the right of center

6. Sew two green sashing strips on either side of a pink print sashing strip. The strip set should measure 5" x 115". Repeat to create a total of 9 of these strip sets. Carefully press sets away from the center strip. Set aside two sashing sets.

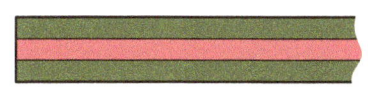

Carolina Lily

Made by Marilyn Mowry of Irving, Texas
Quilted by Sheri Mecom of Bedford, Texas
Finished size: 88" x 88"
Finished block size: 9" x 9"
Blocks needed: 32 full flower blocks, 8 flower-top half blocks, 8 flower-bottom half blocks, and 2 flower-top quarter blocks

7. From the remaining sashing sets, cut two 5" x 90" strips, two 5" x 63" strips, and two 5" x 36" strips. From the remaining partial sets and one 115"-long sashing set, cut two 5" x 11" strips and 39—5" x 9½" strips.

8. Referring to the assembly diagram below, arrange the 32 full flower blocks, 8 flower-top half blocks, 8 flower-bottom half blocks, 2 flower-top quarter blocks, and sashing strips from step 7 (the 39—5" x 9½" strips alternate with the pieced blocks and partial blocks) into rows.

9. Sew the rows from Steps 7 and 8 together, pinning carefully. Please note that each long sashing set is longer than needed. You will trim away the excess AFTER the entire quilt top is assembled. Then press to sashing.

10. Leaving a ¼" seam allowance, trim the excess sashing away from the quilt top. Stay-stitch the entire quilt top perimeter ⅛" from the edge.

11. Quilt, bind, and enjoy. Marilyn's quilt is machine-quilted in a Baptist Fan design.

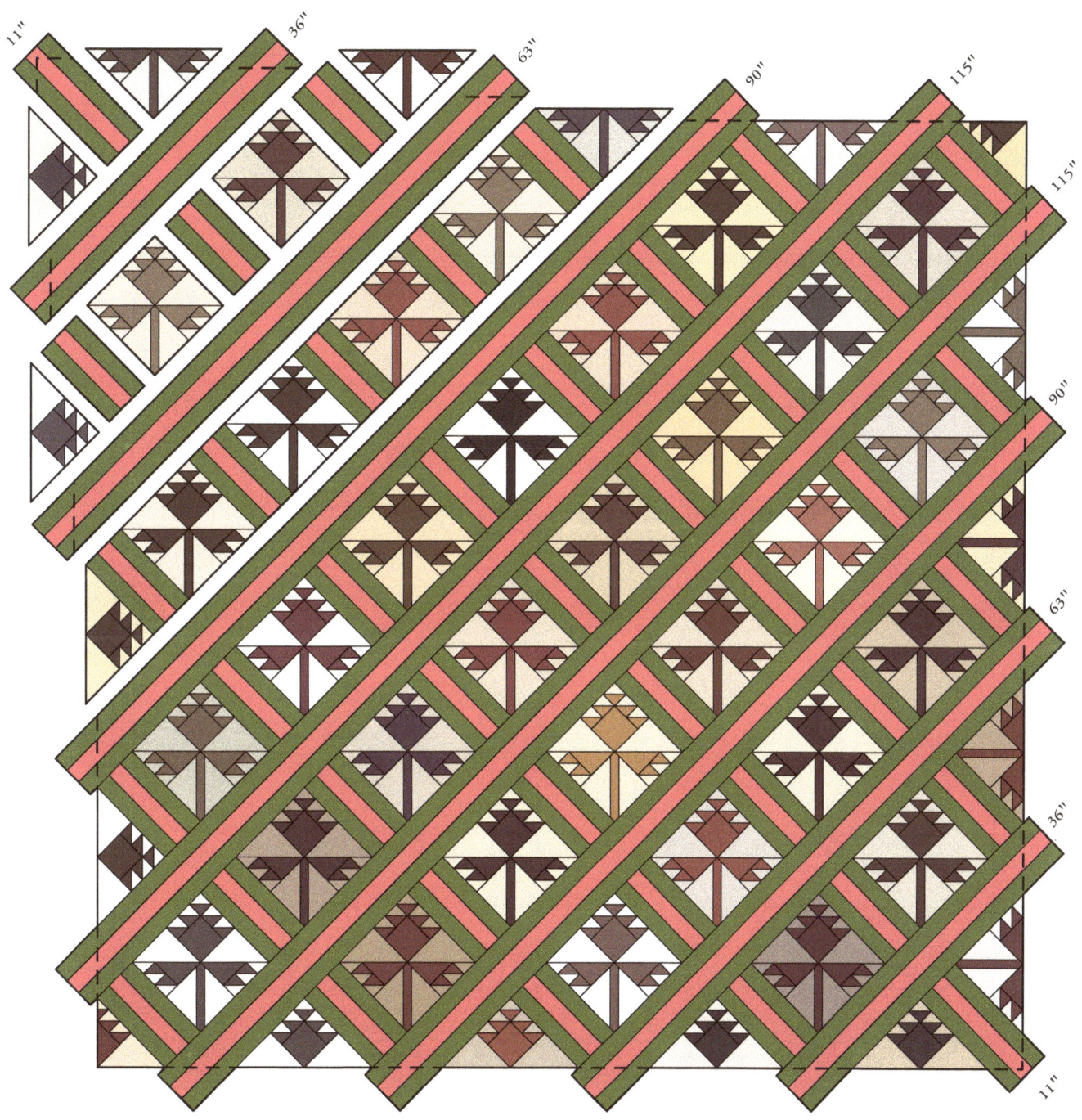

Assembly Diagram

CAROLINA LILY: ON-POINT SET

FABRIC REQUIREMENTS

Blocks:
- 3 yards total of assorted cream to tan prints
- 2½ yards total of assorted brown, madder red, and indigo prints

Setting triangles:
- ½ yard indigo print

Border:
- 2¼ yards madder red print (this is for lengthwise cutting)

Backing:
- 4⅔ yards fabric of your choice

Binding:
- ⅝ yard madder red print

CUTTING INSTRUCTIONS

From assorted cream to tan prints, cut:
- 35—5⅜" squares (A). Then cut once diagonally from corner to corner
- 35—2⅜" squares (B). Then cut once diagonally from corner to corner
- 35—5" squares (C). Then cut once diagonally from corner to corner
- 175—2½" squares (D)

From assorted brown, madder red, and indigo prints, cut:
- 175—2½" squares (D)
- 35—3⅞" squares (E). Then cut once diagonally from corner to corner
- 35—3½" squares (F)
- 35—1⅛" x 7" rectangles (G)

From tan print, cut:
- 3—14" x 14" squares for setting triangles. Then cut squares twice diagonally from corner to corner

From madder red print, cut:
- 4—4½" strips lengthwise for border
- 8—2½" strips the width of fabric for double-fold binding (To give our quilts an antique look, we prefer a 1⅛"-wide single-fold binding. Nineteenth-century quilts often had narrow binding)

SEWING INSTRUCTIONS

1. Referring to the block assembly instructions on page 64, make 31 Carolina Lily blocks.

2. Referring to Steps 2 and 3 on page 64, make four flower-top half blocks.

3. Referring to Steps 4-7 on page 64, make four flower-bottom half blocks.

4. Referring to the assembly diagram on page 73, sew the 31 full blocks, four flower-top half blocks, and four flower-bottom half blocks in diagonal rows.

5. Sew the rows from Step 4 together. The quilt center should measure 59½" x 64¼".

6. Measure through the center of the quilt top from top to bottom and cut two madder red print strips to match that measurement. Sew these two strips to the sides of the quilt top. Then press to border.

7. Measure through the center of the quilt top from side to side and cut two madder red print strips to match that measurement. Sew these two strips to the top and bottom of the quilt top. Press to border.

8. Quilt, bind, and enjoy. Karen quilted in a grid throughout the quilt center and a cable pattern in the border.

Carolina Lily

Pieced and quilted by Karen Hodges of Midlothian, Texas
Finished size: 59½" x 72¼"
Finished block size: 9" x 9"
Number of blocks needed: 31 full blocks, 4 flower-top half blocks,
and 4 flower-bottom half blocks

Assembly Diagram

HISTORY REPEATED

GALLERY

Carolina Lily

Made and hand-quilted by Annette Plog of Arlington, Texas
Approximate finished size: 63" x 84"
24 full blocks, 7 flower-bottom half blocks, 7 flower-top half blocks, and 2 flower-top quarter blocks in a sashed on-point set
Sashing and borders are 2"-wide finished
Quilting: Baptist Fan design with perle cotton

Carolina Lily

Made by Carol Staehle of Arlington, Texas
Machine-quilted by Sheri Mecom of Bedford, Texas
Finished size: 62" x 74"
32 blocks in an on-point set
To showcase the fabric design, the border is 5½"-wide finished
Quilting: Clamshell in quilt center and outline of fabric design in border

CHAPTER 7
BLINDMAN'S FANCY

Inspiration for this February 2008 exchange came from a circa-1880 antique quilt from Canisteo, New York. Made by Marie Boag, it was exhibited at the Buffalo and Erie County Historical Society in 1990. Sixteen participants made one 18" block each for a total of 16 blocks. Fabric selection was limited to 1880s and earlier reproduction fabrics and included checks, stripes, and other visually intriguing prints.

BLINDMAN'S FANCY BLOCK

Finished block size: 18" x 18"

CUTTING INSTRUCTIONS

For each block, cut:

- 1—7¼" square (A) from light, medium, or dark print
- 2—5⅝" squares (B) from assorted light, medium, or dark prints. Then cut squares once diagonally from corner to corner
- 4—2 1/16" squares (C) from assorted light, medium, or dark prints
- 12—2⅝" squares (D) from light print
- 12—2⅝" squares (E) from dark print
- 4—5⅜" squares (F) from assorted light, medium, or dark prints. Then cut squares once diagonally from corner to corner
- 2—5¾" squares (G) from dark print. Then cut squares twice diagonally from corner to corner
- 2—5¾" squares (H) from light print. Then cut squares twice diagonally from corner to corner

BLOCK ASSEMBLY

1. Sew a B triangle to all sides of an A square to create a square-in-square unit. Press away from the center. The unit should measure 10" square unfinished.

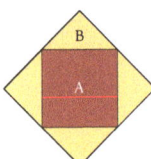

2. Draw a diagonal line once from corner to corner on the wrong side of a D square. With right sides together, layer it on top of an E square. Sew a ¼" seam on both sides of the drawn line. Cut them apart on the drawn line. Press to the dark print. Trim the units to 2 1/16" square unfinished. Make 24 of these units.

3. Sew six half-square triangle units into three rows as shown. Add 2 1/16" squares (C) to opposite ends of two of these rows.

4. Sew six half-square triangle units into one row as shown.

5. Sew the four rows created in Steps 3 and 4 to the sides of the square-in-square unit created in Step 1.

6. Sew a G triangle to an H triangle. Repeat to make a second unit. The resulting hourglass unit should measure 5" square unfinished. Repeat to make three more units.

7. Sew two F triangles to each of the four hourglass units. Press to the triangles.

8. Sew the four corner units from Step 7 to the finished unit from Step 5 to complete the block.

Inspiration Quilt

This circa-1880 antique quilt made in Canisteo, New York, sparked the inspiration for the Blindman's Fancy block exchange.

HISTORY REPEATED

BLINDMAN'S FANCY: STRAIGHT SET

FABRIC REQUIREMENTS

The fabrics needed to make 16 identical blocks are listed in the fabric requirements. To better help you plan your own block exchange, we've specified how much yardage you'll need for each block segment. This is a great project for making use of your fabric stash as almost anything goes.

Blocks:
7¾ yards total of assorted light, medium and dark prints, including:
- ⅞ yard for A
- ⅞ yard for B
- ⅓ yard for C
- 1 yard for D
- 1 yard for E
- 1⅝ yard for F
- 1 yard for G
- 1 yard for H

Flying Geese sashing:
Please note that most of the sashing strips of 12 Flying Geese units use just two different fabrics—one light print and one dark print. To add character to your quilt, you can mix up the look by using more than two prints in some of the strips as shown in the quilt on page 81)
- ⅛ yard each of 32 different light prints
- ⅛ yard each of 32 different dark prints

Flying Geese pink-and-brown side borders:
- ⅝ yard brown print
- ⅝ yard pink print

Two brown borders and one pink border:
- 2⅓ yards brown print
- 1⅛ yards pink print

Backing:
- 10 yards fabric of your choice

Binding:
- 1 yard brown print

CUTTING INSTRUCTIONS

From assorted light, dark, and medium prints, cut:
- 16—7¼" squares (A)
- 32—5⅝" squares (B). Then cut squares once diagonally from corner to corner
- 64—2 1/16" squares (C)
- 192—2⅝" squares (D)
- 192—2⅝" squares (E)
- 64—5⅜" squares (F). Then cut squares once diagonally from corner to corner
- 32—5¾" squares (G). Then cut squares twice diagonally from corner to corner
- 32—5¾" squares (H). Then cut squares twice diagonally from corner to corner

For most of the 12-unit Flying Geese sashing strips that surround the blocks (NOT the two pink and brown side borders), the quilt on page 81 uses just two different fabrics (a light print and a dark print). To add character, you can use more than two fabrics for some of the strips as shown in the featured quilt.

For each 12-unit Flying Geese sashing strip, cut:
- 3—4¼" squares from a light or dark print. Then cut squares twice diagonally for "geese" units
- 12—2⅜" squares from a contrasting print to the one above. Then cut squares once diagonally from corner to corner for "sky" units

From light prints, cut:
- 34—2" squares for four-patch cornerstones (Cut these AFTER your blocks from their leftover scraps)

From dark prints, cut:
- 34—2" squares for four-patch cornerstones (Cut these AFTER your blocks from their leftover scraps)

From pink print, cut:
- 112—2⅜" squares for Flying Geese side borders. Then cut squares once diagonally from corner to corner
- 10—3½" strips the width of fabric for inner pink border

From brown print, cut:
- 28—4¼" squares for Flying Geese side borders. Then cut squares twice diagonally from corner to corner
- 10—3½" strips the width of fabric for inner brown border
- 12—3½" strips the width of fabric for outer brown border
- 13—2½" strips the width of fabric for double-fold binding (To give our quilts an antique look, we prefer 1⅛"-wide single fold binding. Nineteenth-century quilts often had narrow binding)

SEWING INSTRUCTIONS

1. Referring to the block assembly instructions on page 76, make 16 Blindman's Fancy blocks.

2. To create a Flying Geese unit, sew two smaller light print triangles to a larger dark print triangle. Note that some sashing strips have dark "geese" and a light "sky" and others are the opposite.

 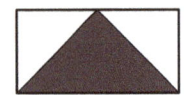

3. Make 32 Flying Geese sashing strips of 12 "geese" each. Press to the "geese" point. Please note the "geese" in the sashing strips do not have to all fly in the same direction. In the inspiration quilt, some of the geese changed directions in the sashing strips.

4. Make 17—3" finished four-patch cornerstones from your leftover scraps from making the blocks.

5. Referring to the assembly diagram on page 82, arrange the Blindman's Fancy blocks, Flying Geese sashing strips, and four-patch sashing cornerstones. Sew the nine rows, then sew all the rows together.

6. For the two pink-and-brown Flying Geese side borders, begin by sewing two pink print triangles to a larger brown print triangle. Repeat to make a total of 112—1½" x 3" finished pink and brown Flying Geese units. Then sew 56 of these units into a row, pressing toward the tip of the "geese" (The number of Flying Geese units in the left side border shown in the photo on page 81 is incorrect. You will need 56 Flying Geese units per side border as specified in our instructions). Referring to the assembly diagram on page 82, add a four-patch block to one end of the strip. Repeat to create a second sashing side border. Sew the two strips to the sides of the quilt top (Please note that the "geese" in the left border are flying down while the "geese" in the right border are flying up).

7. Measure your quilt top through the center from top to bottom. Then join lengths of 3½"-wide brown print strips to match your measurement. Then sew these to the sides of the quilt top and press to the border.

8. Measure your quilt top through the center from side to side. Then join the lengths of 3½"-wide brown print strips to match your measurement. Then sew these to the top and bottom of the quilt top and press to the border.

9. Repeat Steps 7 and 8 for the inner pink print border and the outer brown print border.

10. Quilt, bind, and enjoy. Mary's quilt was machine-quilted in an all-over feather meandering pattern.

Blindman's Fancy

Made by Mary Freeman of Schertz, Texas
Quilted by Fran Le Blanc of San Antonio, Texas
Finished size: 105" x 105"
Finished block size: 18" x 18"
Number of blocks needed: 16

Assembly Diagram

GALLERY

Blindman's Fancy

Made by Carol Staehle of Arlington, Texas
Quilted by Sheri Mecom of Bedford, Texas
Finished size: 60" x 81"
12 blocks in a Flying-Geese sashed straight set
Quilting: Baptist Fan

Blindman's Fancy

Made by Deb Otto of Euless, Texas
Quilted by Sheri Mecom of Bedford, Texas
Finished size: 87" x 87"
16 blocks in a sashed straight set
Sashing features hourglass cornerstones
Quilting: Feathered wreath designs in blocks and leaf pattern in sashing

HISTORY REPEATED 83

Fancy Blind Geese

Made by Linda Cordell Wilkey of Mathis, Texas
Quilted by Dawn Smith of Grapevine, Texas
Finished size: 75" x 94"
12 blocks in a Flying-Geese sashed straight set
Each of the three blue outer borders are 2"-wide finished
for a 6"-wide finished overall border area
Quilting: All-over feather meandering

Blindman's Fancy

Made by Peggy Faubert Morton of Boerne, Texas
Hand-quilted by Elizabeth A. Miller of Caston, Wisconsin
Finished size: 89" x 111"
20 blocks in a Flying-Geese sashed straight set
Quilting: In-the-ditch

Blindman's Fancy

Made by Marilyn Mowry of Irving, Texas
Quilted by Sheri Mecom of Bedford, Texas
Finished size: 87" x 87"
16 blocks in a sashed straight set
3"-wide finished sashing and 3" square finished cornerstones
Quilting: All-over Baptist Fan variation

CHAPTER 8
WHEEL of FORTUNE

Inspiration for this 2008 block exchange was an 1877 antique quilt owned by Bobbie Aug. Called the "Peaceful Valley Quilt", it was pictured in her book, *Vintage Quilts*. Eighteen participants exchanged two blocks each for a total of 36 blocks. Fabric selection for block backgrounds ranged from small-print creams to light tans or shirtings with black or brown motifs. For the stars, we specified that no neons, clarets, or cadet blues be used.

WHEEL OF FORTUNE BLOCK

Finished block size: 8¾" x 8¾"

CUTTING INSTRUCTIONS

For one block, cut:
- 4—2½" squares (A) from assorted light prints
- 8—1⅞" x 2½" rectangles (B) from assorted light prints
- 2—3½" squares (C) from assorted light prints. Then cut squares twice diagonally from corner to corner
- 4—1⅞" squares (D) from assorted light prints
- 8—1⅞" squares (E) from assorted dark prints
- 2—3½" squares (F) from assorted dark prints. Then cut squares twice diagonally from corner to corner
- 1—5¼" square (G) from dark print

BLOCK ASSEMBLY

1. Sew two C triangles to two F triangles to create a quarter-square triangle unit. Repeat to make a total of four of these units. Trim units to 2½" square.

2. With right sides together, layer a 1⅞" dark print square (E) on top of the right side of a 1⅞" x 2½" rectangle (B). Then stitch from corner to corner as shown. Press to dark fabric and trim a ¼" seam allowance to the two layers below. Repeat to make a total of 4 of these units.

3. With right sides together, layer a 1⅞" dark print square (E) on top of the right side of a 1⅞" x 2½" rectangle (B). Then stitch from corner to corner as shown. Press to dark print and trim a ¼" seam allowance to the two layers below. Repeat to make a total of four of these units.

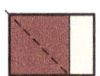

4. With right sides together, layer a 1⅞" light print square (D) on top of one corner of a 5¼" dark print square (G). Then sew diagonally across the light print square as shown below. Cut the corner, leaving a ¼" seam allowance. Then press the triangle open toward the light print. Repeat this for the remaining three corners of the 5¼" dark print square.

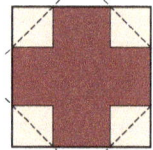 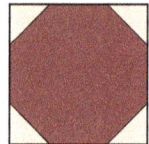

5. Referring to the top row in the following diagram, sew the following units together in this order: a 2½" light print square (A), a unit from Step 2, a quarter-square triangle unit, a unit from Step 3, and a 2½" light print square (A). Repeat to create a second row.

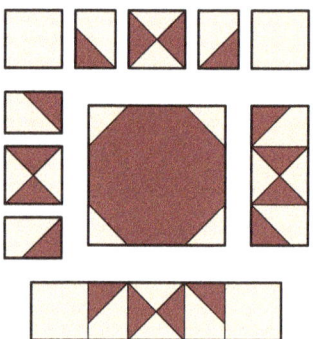

6. Referring to the middle row in the previous diagram, sew a unit from Step 2 to the left side of a quarter-square triangle unit and a unit from Step 3 to its right. Repeat to create a second row. Then sew these two completed rows to opposite sides of the unit from Step 4.

7. Join the three rows from Steps 5 and 6 to complete the block.

WHEEL OF FORTUNE: ZIGZAG SET

FABRIC REQUIREMENTS

Blocks:
- 2¾ yards total of assorted light prints
- 2¾ yards total of assorted dark prints

Setting triangles:
- 3 yards cheddar print

Backing:
- 5 yards fabric of your choice

Binding:
- ¾ yard cheddar print

CUTTING INSTRUCTIONS

From assorted light prints, cut:
- 128—2½" squares (A)
- 256—1⅞" x 2½" rectangles (B)
- 64—3½" squares (C). Then cut squares twice diagonally from corner to corner
- 128—1⅞" squares (D)

From assorted dark prints, cut:
- 256—1⅞" squares (E)
- 64—3½" squares (F). Then cut squares twice diagonally from corner to corner
- 32—5¼" squares (G)

From cheddar print, cut:
- 14—14" squares for setting triangles. Then cut squares twice diagonally from corner to corner
- 6—7¼" squares for corner triangles. Then cut squares once diagonally from corner to corner
- 8—2½" strips the width of fabric for double-fold binding (To give our quilts an antique look, we prefer a 1⅛"-wide single-fold binding. Nineteenth-century quilts often had narrow binding)

SEWING INSTRUCTIONS

1. Referring to the block assembly instructions on page 86, sew 32 Wheel of Fortune blocks.

2. Cut four of the Wheel of Fortune blocks a ¼" to the right of the center to accommodate a seam allowance. Then stay-stitch the bias edge. You will only use the section with the ¼" seam allowance.

Cut ¼" to the right of center

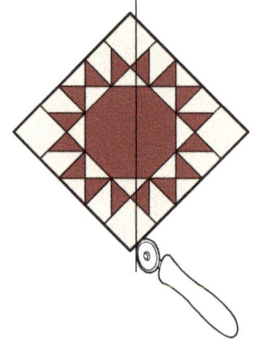

3. Sew six blocks, 10 setting triangles, and four corner triangles to create a row. Repeat to make a total of three rows. Press to the setting triangles.

4. Sew five blocks, two half blocks, and 12 setting triangles to create a row. Repeat to make a total of two rows. Press to the setting triangles.

A Cheddar Wheel

Made by Betty Edgell of Colleyville, Texas
Quilted by Sheri Mecom of Bedford, Texas
Finished size: 61⅞" x 74¾"
Finished block size: 8¾" x 8¾"
Number of blocks needed: 32

HISTORY REPEATED 89

5. Trim the long sides of the five rows created in Steps 3 and 4 to accommodate a ¼" seam allowance.

6. Referring to the assembly diagram below, sew the five rows together.

7. Quilt, bind, and enjoy. The zigzag setting in Betty's quilt features trailing feathers.

Assembly Diagram

WHEEL OF FORTUNE: GARDEN MAZE SET

FABRIC REQUIREMENTS

Blocks:
- 3 yards total of assorted light prints
- 2¾ yards total of assorted dark prints

Sashing:
- 2¼ yards green print
- 2 yards brown print

Backing:
- 4½ yards fabric of your choice

Binding:
- ¾ yard brown and madder red print

CUTTING INSTRUCTIONS

From assorted light prints, cut:
- 144—2½" squares (A)
- 288—1⅞" x 2½" rectangles (B)
- 72—3½" squares (C). Then cut squares twice diagonally from corner to corner
- 144—1⅞" squares (D)

From assorted dark prints, cut:
- 288—1⅞" squares (E)
- 72—3½" squares (F). Then cut squares twice diagonally from corner to corner
- 36—5¼" squares (G)

From green print, cut:
- 5—9¼" the width of fabric strips for sashing. Then sub-cut into 84—2¼" x 9¼" strips

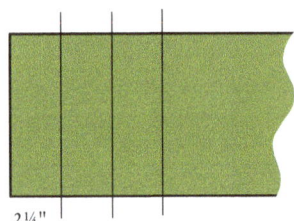

- 49—3½" squares for sashing cornerstone cross backgrounds. Then cut squares twice diagonally from corner to corner

From brown print, cut:
- 5—9¼" strips the width of fabric for sashing. Then sub-cut into 168—1⅛" x 9¼" strips

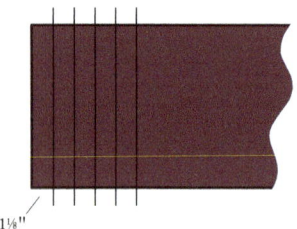

- 49—1⅜" x 5¼" strips for sashing cornerstone crosses
- 98—1⅜" x 2½" strips for sashing cornerstone crosses

From brown and madder print, cut:
- 8—2½" strips the width of fabric for double-fold binding (To give our quilts an antique look, we prefer a 1⅛"-wide single-fold binding. Nineteenth-century quilts often had narrow binding)

SEWING INSTRUCTIONS

1. Referring to the block assembly instructions on page 86, make 36 Wheel of Fortune blocks.

2. Sew two 1⅛" x 9¼" brown print sashing strips to opposite sides of a 2¼" x 9¼" green print sashing strip. Repeat to make a total of 84 of these strip sets.

3. Sew two green print triangles cut from G squares to opposite sides of a 1⅜" x 2½" brown print sashing cornerstone cross strip. Repeat to create a second unit.

4. Sew two units from Step 3 to opposite sides of a 1⅜" x 5½" brown print sashing cornerstone cross strip. Trim the cornerstone to 3½" square.

5. Repeat Steps 3 and 4 to create a total of 49 cornerstone crosses.

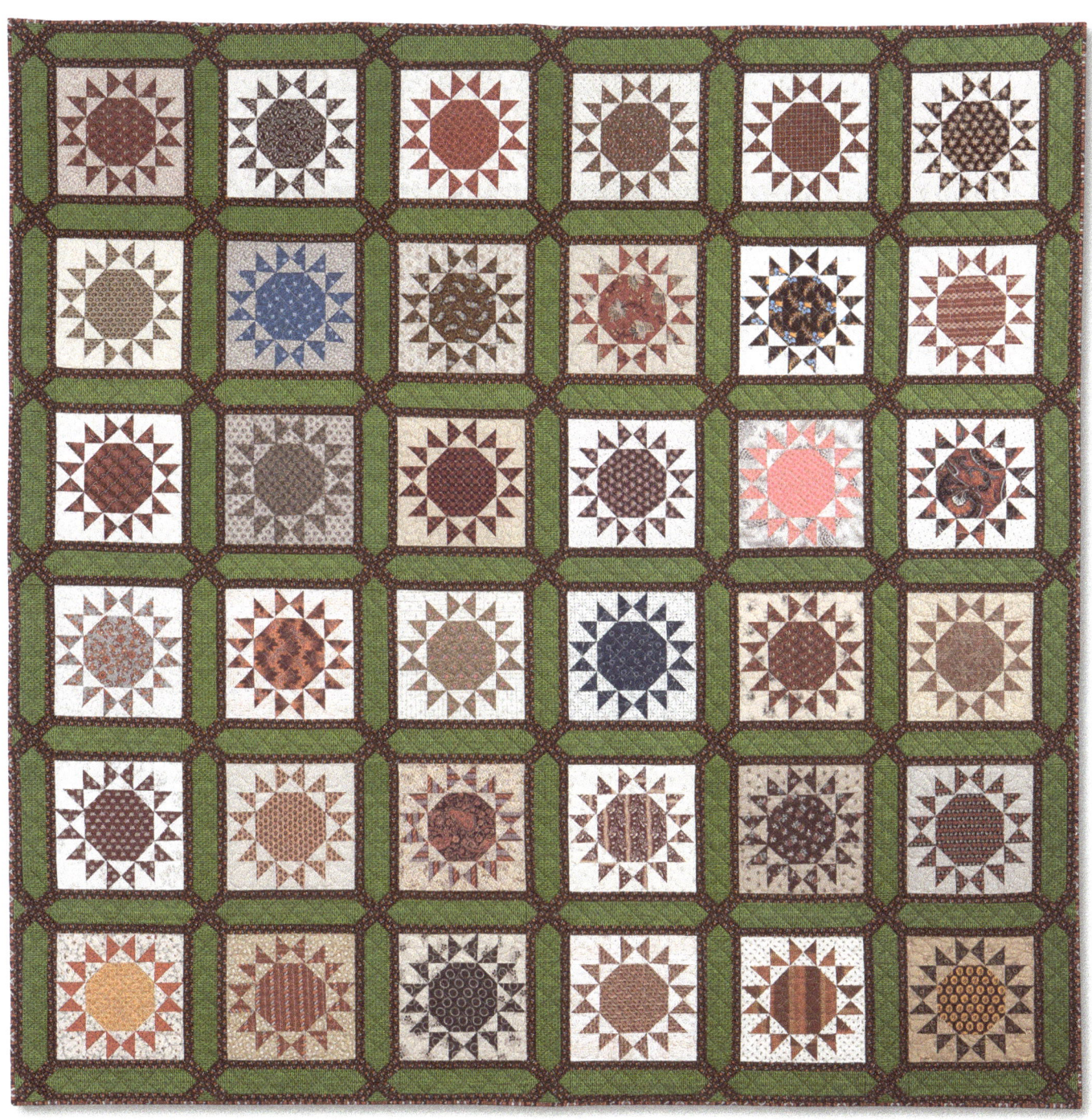

A Fortunate Garden

Made by Betsy Chutchian of Grand Prairie, Texas
Quilted by Sheri Mecom of Bedford, Texas
Finished size: 75½" x 73½"
Finished block size: 8¾" x 8¾"
Blocks needed: 36

6. Sew six Wheel of Fortune blocks to seven sashing strips, beginning and ending with a sashing strip. Repeat to create a total of six rows.

7. Sew six sashing strips to seven cornerstone crosses, beginning and ending with a cornerstone cross. Repeat to create a total of seven rows.

8. Referring to the assembly diagram below, join the 13 rows from Steps 6 and 7.

9. Quilt, bind, and enjoy. Betsy's quilt features a feathered wreath in each block and crosshatching in the sashing strips. The brown strips in the sashing and in the sashing cornerstone crosses are quilted through the center of each strip.

Assembly Diagram

GALLERY

Spin the Wheel

Made by Ramona Bailey Williams of Missouri City, Texas
Quilted by Melba Drennan of Pearland, Texas
Finished size: 61¾" x 79¼"
33 blocks in a medallion set
Squares and half-square triangles are 2 3/16" finished (or 2⅛" with scant seams)

Cheddar Wheel

Made by Karen Hodges of Midlothian, Texas
Quilted by Susan Corbett of Fort Worth, Texas
Finished size: 79¾" x 109¼"
35 blocks in a straight set
Sashing strips are 1½"-wide finished and the nine-patch cornerstones are 3"-wide finished
Quilting: Cable design in sashing

HISTORY REPEATED 95

Wheel of Fortune 👉

Made by Carol Staehle of Arlington, Texas
Quilted by Sheri Mecom of Bedford, Texas
Finished size: 67⅜" x 79¾"
28 blocks and 4 half blocks in a zigzag set
Borders are 5½"-wide finished
Quilting: Feathered wreaths in blocks and feathers in zigzag sections

👉 Wheel of Fortune

Made by Peggy Fauger Morton of Bourne, Texas
Hand-quilted by Elizabeth Miller of Caston, Wisconsin
Finished size: 94½" x 112½"
50 blocks in a straight set
Inner border is 1½"-wide finished, side border is 6"-wide finished, and top and bottom borders are 7"-wide finished

Golden Sunset 👉

Made by Jean Johnson of Murphy, Texas
Quilted by Sheri Mecom of Bedford, Texas
Finished size: 74½" x 88"
30 blocks in an on-point set
Quilting: Feathered wreaths in blocks and setting triangles and a feathered design in border

CHAPTER 9
CHEDDAR TRIANGLES

Inspiration for this June 2009 block exchange came from a photo of a unique quilt top owned by Miriam Kujac of Madrid, Iowa. It was published in the October 2008 issue of *American Patchwork and Quilting* magazine. Seventeen participants exchanged eight blocks per person for a total of 136 blocks. We used 1880s and earlier reproduction fabrics in brown, blue, indigo, Prussian blue, Perkins purple, pink, Turkey red, and green as well as light and medium shirtings and conversational prints. All participants used the same cheddar fabric. We did not use poison greens, neons, clarets, chrome yellows, or cadet blues.

CHEDDAR TRIANGLES BLOCK

Finished block size: 6" x 6"

CUTTING INSTRUCTIONS

For each scrappy block (consisting of nine half-square triangle units), cut:

- 9—2⅞" squares (A) from dark prints. Then cut squares diagonally from corner to corner. You will use nine of the triangles
- 8—2⅞" squares (B) from light or medium prints. Then cut squares once diagonally from corner to corner. You will use eight of the triangles
- 1—2⅞" square (C) from solid cheddar print. Then cut square once diagonally from corner to corner. You will use one of the triangles

BLOCK ASSEMBLY

1. Make eight scrappy half-square triangle units using eight A triangles and eight B triangles.

2. Make one scrappy half-square triangle unit using one A triangle and one C cheddar print triangle.

3. Sew the units from Steps 1 and 2 into three rows. Then sew the rows together. To reduce bulk when assembling the top, press the seams open.

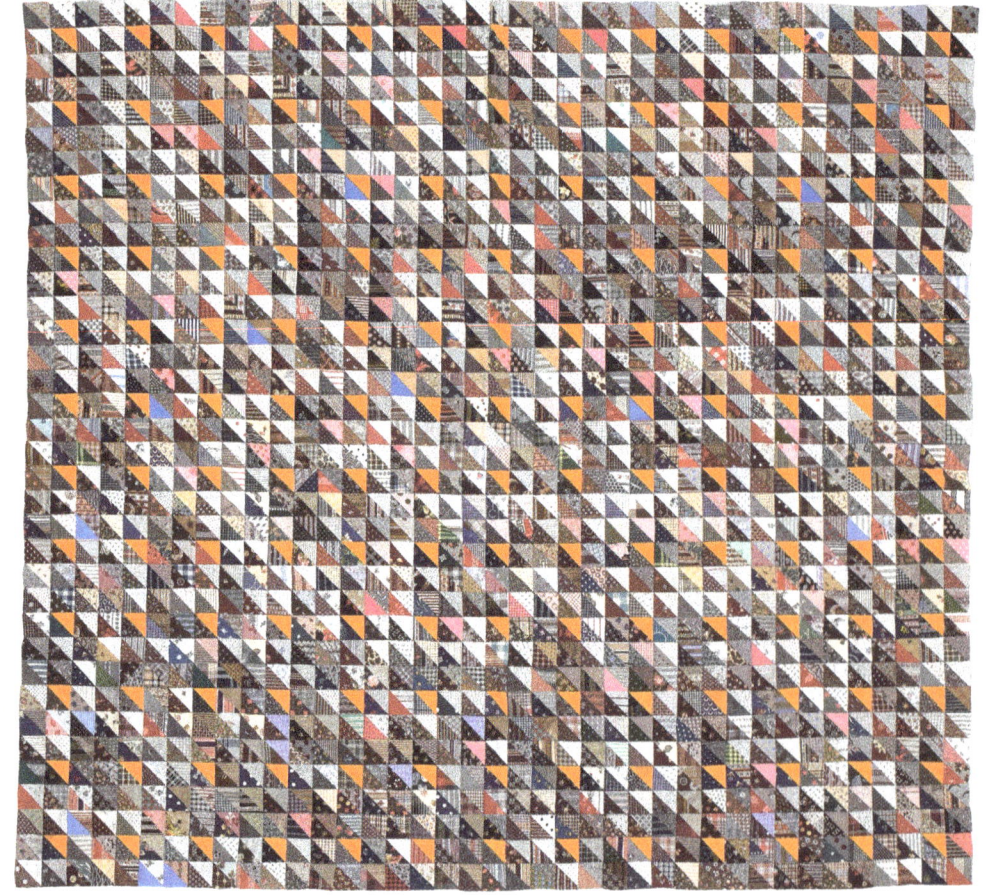

This antique quilt top owned by avid quilt collector Miriam Kujac of Madrid, Iowa, inspired the Cheddar Triangles block exchange. Miriam found the top in Farmington, Connecticut.

CHEDDAR TRIANGLES: ON-POINT SET

FABRIC REQUIREMENTS

Blocks:
- 1½ yards total of assorted dark prints
- 1⅓ yards total of assorted light and medium prints
- ⅜ yard cheddar solid

Sashing and cornerstones:
- 2½ yards red print
- 3 yards light print

Setting triangles and corner triangles:
- 1½ yards cheddar print

Backing:
- 5 yards fabric of your choice

Binding:
- ⅔ yard red print

CUTTING INSTRUCTIONS

From assorted dark prints, cut:
- 225—2⅞" squares (A). Then cut squares diagonally from corner to corner

From assorted light and medium prints, cut:
- 200—2⅞" squares (B). Then cut squares once diagonally from corner to corner

From cheddar solid, cut:
- 50—2⅞" squares (C). Then cut squares once diagonally from corner to corner

From cheddar print, cut:
- 5—14" squares for setting triangles. Then cut squares twice diagonally from corner to corner
- 2—9⅜" squares for corner triangles. Then cut squares once diagonally from corner to corner

From red print, cut:
- 120—4¼" squares for Flying Geese units. Then cut squares twice diagonally from corner to corner
- 71—3½" squares for square-in-square sashing cornerstones
- 8—2½" strips the width of fabric for double-fold binding (To give our quilts an antique look, we prefer a 1⅛" single fold binding. Nineteenth-century quilts often had narrow binding)

From light prints, cut:
- 480—2⅜" squares for Flying Geese units. Then cut squares once diagonally from corner to corner
- 284—2" squares for square-in-a-square sashing cornerstones

SEWING INSTRUCTIONS

1. Referring to the block assembly instructions on page 98, make 50 Cheddar Triangles blocks.

2. To create a Flying Geese unit, sew two light print triangles cut from the 2⅜" squares to a larger red print triangle cut from the 4¼" squares. Repeat to make a total of 480 Flying Geese units. Press to the light print triangles.

 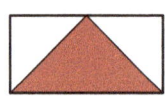

3. Sew four Flying Geese units together to form one sashing unit. Repeat for a total of 120 units. Press to the "geese" points.

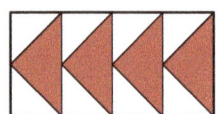

4. To create a square-in-a-square unit, begin by drawing a diagonal line from corner to corner on one 2" light print square. With right sides together, layer the marked 2" light print square on one corner of a 3½" red print square. Sew on the drawn line. Press to the corner and trim away excess fabric below. Repeat this process for the remaining three corners.

5. Repeat Step 4 to make a total of 71 square-in-a-square units.

6. Referring to the assembly diagram on page 102, arrange the 50 Cheddar Triangles blocks, 120 Flying Geese sashing strips, 71 square-in-square sashing cornerstones, 28 setting triangles, and four corner triangles in diagonal rows. Then sew the rows together and join the rows.

7. Quilt, bind, and enjoy. Mary's quilt was custom machine-quilted in a Baptist Fan design.

Cheddar Geese

Made by Mary Freeman of Schertz, Texas
Quilted by Sandra Towey of Schertz, Texas
Finished size: 68" x 80¾"
Finished block size: 6" x 6"
Number of blocks needed: 50

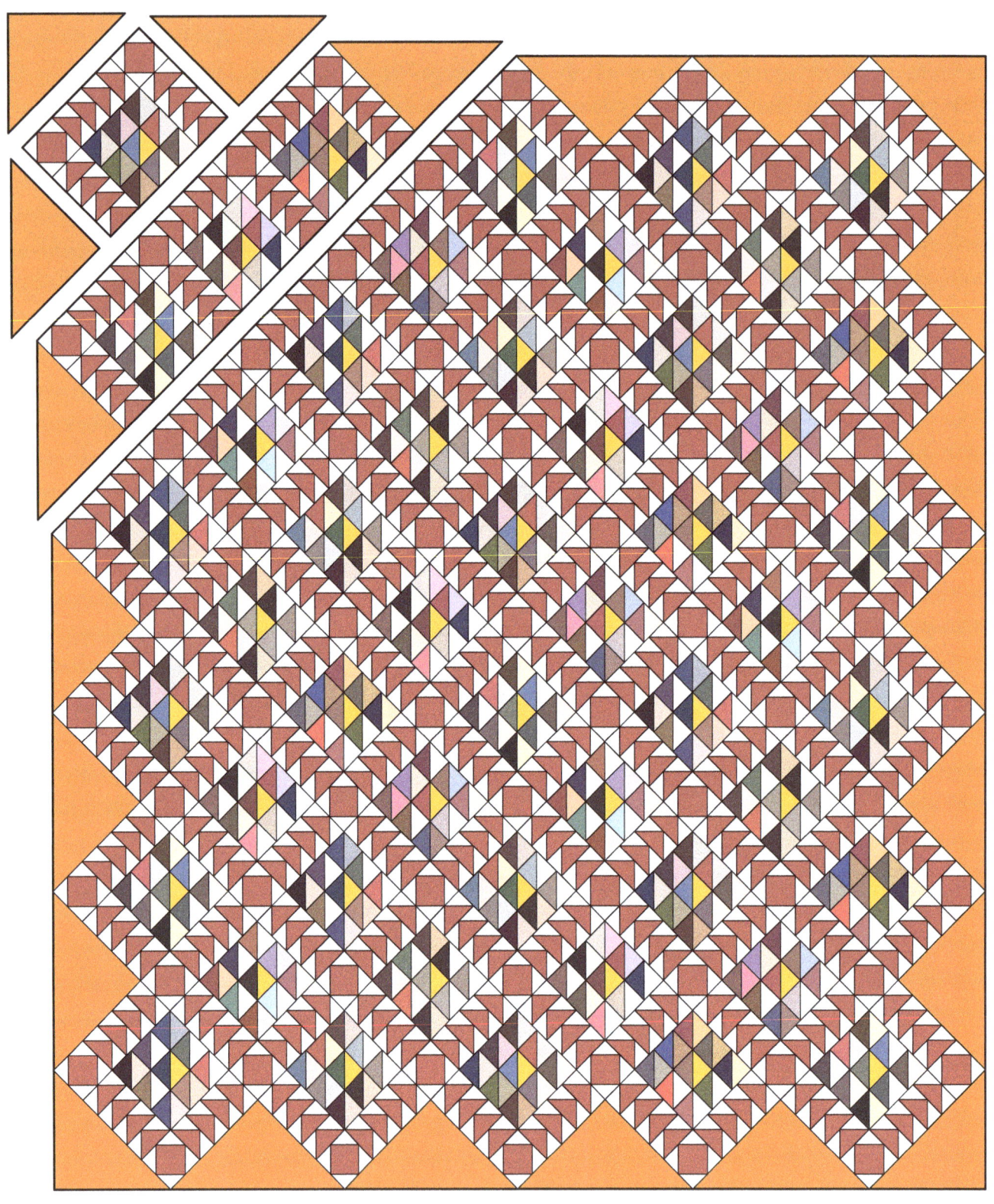

Assembly Diagram

GALLERY

Cheddar Triangles

Made by Deb Otto of Euless, Texas
Quilted by Dawn Smith of Grapevine, Texas
Finished size: 68" x 78"
130 blocks in a strippy set
Strips are 2"-wide finished
Quilting: All-over feather meandering

Cheddar Triangles

Made by Peggy Fauber Morton of Boerne, Texas
Hand-quilted by Katie Fisher of Kinzer, Pennsylvania
Finished size: 92" x 113"
154 Cheddar Triangles blocks and 54 Log Cabin blocks in a straight set
Log Cabin blocks are 7" square finished and sashing and cornerstones are 1"-wide finished
Quilting: In-the-ditch

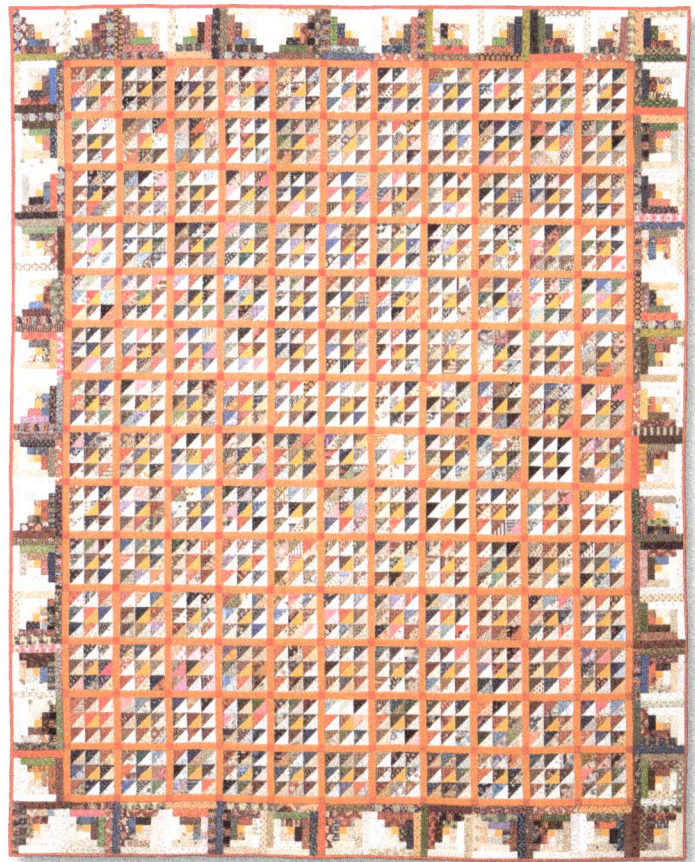

HISTORY REPEATED 103

Santa Fe Sunlight

Made by Janet Henderson of Fort Worth, Texas
Quilted by Sheri Mecom of Bedford, Texas
Finished size: 60" x 72"
120 blocks set in four quadrants of five blocks across and six down
Quilting: Diagonal lines accentuate the quadrants

Cheddar Triangles

Made and hand-quilted by Wanda Hetrick of Arlington, Texas
Finished size: 81" x 90"
165 blocks in a strippy set
Strips are 3"-wide finished
Quilting: All-over grid pattern

Cheddar Triangles

Made by Annette Plog of Arlington, Texas
Quilted by Sheri Mecom of Bedford, Texas
Finished size: 60" x 72"
120 blocks in a straight set
Quilting: All-over Baptist Fan design

104 HISTORY REPEATED

CHAPTER 10
OHIO STARS

Inspiration for this December 2009 block exchange came from a photo in a calendar called Heirloom Quilts, published by Golden Turtle Press. The quilt was dated 1880-1890 and made in Illinois by an unknown quilter. We were intrigued by the unique corners and the number of pieces in each block. Twenty-one participants exchanged one block each for 21 total blocks. Fabric selection was 1850-1880 reproduction prints. No floral, conversational, neon, or claret fabrics were to be used since they weren't in the antique quilt. We chose small- to medium-scale prints in light medium, medium, and dark shades.

OHIO STARS BLOCK

Finished block size: 12" x 12"

CUTTING INSTRUCTIONS

For each block, cut: (The blocks are scrappy so you don't need to use specific types of prints for the following segments)

- 2—5¼" squares (A). Then cut squares twice diagonally from corner to corner
- 2—5¼" squares (B). Then cut squares twice diagonally from corner to corner
- 20—1½" x 2½" rectangles (C)
- 20—1½" squares (D)
- 5—1⅞" squares (E)
- 10—2" squares (F). Then cut squares once diagonally from corner to corner

BLOCK ASSEMBLY

1. To create an hourglass unit, sew two A triangles and two B triangles. Then trim to 4½" square. Repeat to create a total of 4 of these blocks.

2. To create a square-in-square unit, sew four triangles cut from 2" squares (F) to the four sides of a 1⅞" square (E).

3. Referring to the top and bottom rows in the diagram below, sew a 1½" square (D) to opposite sides of a 1½" x 2½" rectangle (C). Repeat to create a second row.

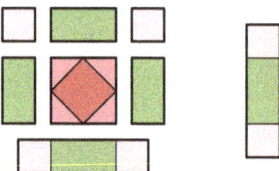

4. Referring to the middle row in the previous diagram, sew a 1½" x 2½" rectangle (C) to both sides of a square-in-a-square unit from Step 2. Sew the three rows from this and the previous step together to complete the block. Repeat to create a total of five of these blocks.

5. Sew two blocks from Step 4 to opposite sides of an hourglass unit. Repeat to make a total of two of these rows.

6. Sew two hourglass units to opposite sides of a block from Step 4.

7. Join the three rows from Steps 5 and 6 to complete the block.

OHIO STARS: STRAIGHT SET

FABRIC REQUIREMENTS

Blocks:
- 6½ yards total of assorted light, medium, and dark prints, including:
    - 1⅜ yards for A
    - 1⅜ yards for B
    - 1¼ yards for C
    - ¾ yard for D
    - ⅜ yard for E
    - ⅔ yard for F

Sashing and inner border:
- ⅓ yard assorted light and dark prints each for hourglass sashing cornerstones (G and H)
- 1¾ yards red print for sashing strips
- ¼ yard light stripe for inner border squares and rectangles

Outer border:
- 2½ yards red plaid (This is for lengthwise OR mitered cutting)

Backing:
- 7½ yards fabric of your choice

Binding:
- ⅔ yards red print

CUTTING INSTRUCTIONS

From assorted prints, cut:
- 90—5¼" squares (A). Then cut squares twice diagonally from corner to corner
- 90—5¼" squares (B). Then cut squares twice diagonally from corner to corner
- 440—1½" x 2½" rectangles (C)
- 440—1½" squares (D)
- 110—1⅞" squares (E)
- 220—2" squares (F). Then cut squares once diagonally from corner to corner
- 10—3¼" squares (G) for hourglass sashing cornerstones. Then cut squares twice diagonally from corner to corner
- 10—3¼" squares (H) for hourglass sashing cornerstones. Then cut squares twice diagonally from corner to corner

From red print, cut:
- 3—12½" strips the width of fabric for sashing strips. Then sub-cut these strips into 41—2½" x 12½" strips

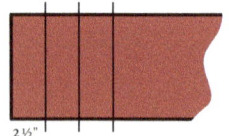

- 1—12½" strip the width of fabric for inner border strips. Then sub-cut the strip into 18—1½" x 12½" strips

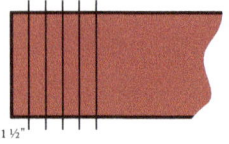

- 8—2½" x 4½" strips
- 4—1½" x 4½" strips
- 9—2½" strips the width of fabric for double-fold binding (To give our quilts an antique look, we prefer 1⅛" single-fold binding. Nineteenth-century quilts often had narrow binding)

From red plaid, cut:
- 4—6½"-wide strips lengthwise for outer border

From light stripe, cut:
- 4—1½" x 1½" squares for inner border corners
- 18—1½" x 2½" rectangles for inner border

SEWING INSTRUCTIONS

1. Referring to the block assembly instructions on page 106, make 20 Ohio Stars blocks, 20 additional hourglass units, and 10 additional square-in-a-square units for partial blocks.

2. Sew 10 partial blocks by sewing two hourglass units to opposite sides of a square-in-square unit.

3. Referring to Step 1 in the block assembly instructions on page 106, make 20 hourglass cornerstones with triangles G and H. Then trim the units to measure 2½" square.

4. Referring to the assembly diagram on page 109, arrange the full blocks, partial blocks, sashing strips, sashing cornerstones, sashing squares, and sashing rectangles into rows.

5. Referring to the assembly diagram, join the 13 rows.

6. Measure your quilt top through the center from top to bottom. Then cut two lengths of 6½"-wide red plaid strips to match your measurement (Instead of cutting the strips to fit, Linda chose to miter the borders to better showcase the plaid fabric). Then sew these to the sides of the quilt top and press to the border.

7. Measure your quilt top through the center from side to side. Then cut two lengths of 6½"-wide red plaid strips to match your measurement (Instead of cutting the strips to fit, Linda chose to miter the borders to better showcase the plaid fabric). Then sew these to the top and bottom of the quilt top and press to the border.

8. Quilt, bind, and enjoy. Linda's quilt features feather designs in the border.

Assembly Diagram

Ohio Stars

Made by Linda Cordell Wilkey of Mathis, Texas
Quilted by Dana Goyer of Euless, Texas
Finished size: 80" x 82"
Finished block size: 12" x 12"
Blocks needed: 20 full and 10 partial blocks

GALLERY

Ohio Stars

Made and hand-quilted by Ann Jernigan of Arlington, Texas
Finished size: 65" x 85"
20 blocks and 4 partial blocks in a sashed straight set
Sashing is 1½"-wide finished, inner border is 1"-wide finished, and outer border is 4½"-wide finished
Quilting: Baptist Fan design

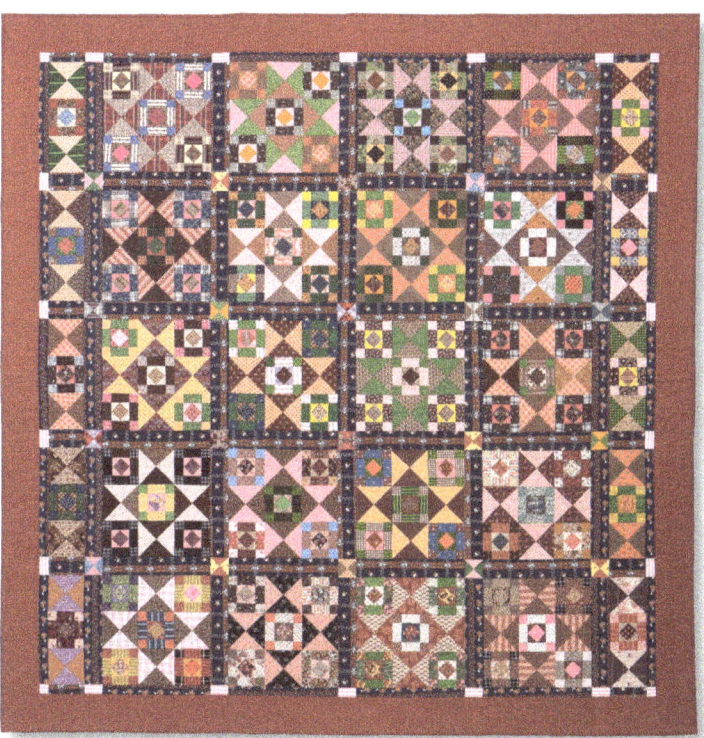

Ohio Stars

Made by Carol Staehle of Arlington, Texas
Quilted by Sheri Mecom of Bedford, Texas
Finished size: 76" x 78"
20 blocks and 10 partial blocks in a sashed straight set
Sashing is 2"-wide finished, inner border is 1"-wide finished, and outer border is 4"-wide finished

Stars over Green Pastures

Made by Mary Freeman of Schertz, Texas
Quilted by Sandra Towery of Schertz, Texas
Finished size: 68" x 90"
18 blocks in a sashed on-point set
Sawtooth setting triangles
Quilting: Custom-quilted feathers

Alice T. Harvey made this hand-quilted signature quilt, **"Remembrance"**, as part of our second signature block exchange in 2006. Normally we do not exchange appliqué blocks, but a few of our members volunteered to make them for this exchange. Another signature quilt is in our future.

www.ingramcontent.com/pod-product-compliance
Lightning Source LLC
Chambersburg PA
CBHW051550220426
43671CB00024B/2993